"What an intriguing and interesting read this dialogue is between two Jungian analysts! It is the deep psychic perception of small-large events, simple but extraordinary, that both of them experienced and have remained etched into their memories the quicksilver of a significant correpondence about the exceptional experience of the Nobel winning physicist Wolfgang Pauli which allows us to participate in their own personal and clinical experience."

– Daniela Iorio, CIPA

"Elena and Murray's choice of correspondence to illustrate an intensely shared observation pleasantly reminds us of other times and other literature that have formed us. The authors' courageous research, while implicitly emphasising the constraints of today's physicalism, paves the way for a theory that "in another era" would integrate and unify physics and depth psychology, causality and synchronicity, subject and object, temporality and timelessness. How can we not be grateful to Elena and Murray for this vital and inspiring perspective about sense and unity?"

– Anna Panepucci, AIPA and IAAP

"One never tires of exploring the wonderful mind of Wolfgang Pauli! This remarkable book, incorporating a real e-mail exchange between its two authors begins in one of Pauli's active imaginations. The outcome includes the introduction of a new and original notion of 'dyschronicity'. This adds something to the literature on 'time'. But then something a little mysterious happens – and I think it is the result of the relational dialogue itself and the human connection between the two people – and the conversation moves into a focus on 'evil'. The twinning of 'time' and 'evil' is extremely challenging for any reader but, having considered it, I found it illuminating. And that is hard to find in today's Jungian field, wherein 'evil' comes dangerously close to being done to death. Not in this volume, though!"

– Andrew Samuels, University of Essex, UK

"The experience of *time*, confrontations with *evil*, the role of the ego in the *realization of the Self*: three basic threads that run through the works of Jung and emerge as determining factors in his more mature thought and in his later works. These, along with the question of *shame*, are artfully and thoughtfully delved into by two analysts with years of experience in clinical work. The experience of time (and of timelessness) is examined by Murray Stein in light of four types of experience called by the author "cronicity", "acronicity", "synchronicity" and "dischronicity" while both Stein and Caramazza reflect on the problem of evil and on its relation to divinity from various points of view. Their profound reflections which draw on science, philosophy, theology and clinical psychology are woven together and make for a highly stimulating and rewarding read. The book, which contains articles by Murray Stein previously published in magazines and journals as well as passages taken from a volume published by Elena Caramazza on the theme of evil and suffering, is a small but extremely rich compendium of reflections on essential questions. A dialogue between two thinking souls who never shy away from sharing personal experience; it will nourish the soul of anyone looking for a serious, feeling treatment of these deep and, at times, disturbing issues of human existence."

– Robert M. Mercurio, training analyst ARPA, Rome, Italy

"The extraordinary topicality of this volume can only be grasped by answering the following question: what political and ideological force holds sway in these current times? Socialist solidarity and nationalistic aggressiveness have been jettisoned and the new stance adopted by the 21st-century leader never ceases to amaze: he is "shameless." What appeared to be a personal virtue has become, through its absence, a major form of political leverage. The leader can hurl insults or tell lies: to hell with his program, he must lead the dance.

Two of the most highly respected exponents of the Jungian world explore the theme of shame, placing it in the necessary contexts: time, the experience of analysis, and ethics which can never be reduced to a body of rules. Rather than being tasked with eliminating evil as an obstacle, ethics is translated into an eternal struggle."

– Luigi Zoja, analytical psychologist, Milan, Italy

Temporality, Shame, and the Problem of Evil in Jungian Psychology

In a unique epistolary style, authors Murray Stein and Elena Caramazza share their rich and reflective conversations surrounding the themes of temporality, shame, and evil through letters, essays, and email correspondence. Ignited by Wolfgang Pauli's "The Piano Lesson," Stein and Caramazza study the function of temporality and consider the importance of shame and evil to this relationship. In this book Stein shows how Pauli, as a result of his contact with C.G. Jung and analytical psychology, embarked on a thought experiment to merge two currents of scientific thought: quantum physics and depth psychology.

In his work of active imagination "The Piano Lesson," Pauli playfully brings together the former, which supplies a causal explanation of the mechanics of the material world, and the latter, which supplies an approach to meaning. The problem of how to merge the two currents in one language is presented in Pauli's symbolic solution, piano music, which combines the black and white keys in a single harmony. This music symbolizes a unified theory that combines the explanations of causality and the meaning delivered by synchronicity.

Presenting an original approach to synchronicity and dis-synchronicity, this interdisciplinary and innovative exchange concludes with a script written by Murray Stein, inspired by Pauli, as well as an afterword by influential Jungian scholars. This book will be a key reference for undergraduate and postgraduate courses and seminars in Jungian and post-Jungian studies, philosophy, psychoanalytic studies, psychology, and the social sciences.

Murray Stein, PhD, was president of the International Association for Analytical Psychology from 2001 to 2004 and President of The International School of Analytical Psychology in Zurich from 2008 to 2012. He is the author of *Minding the Self*, editor with Lucy Huskinson of *Analytical Psychology in a Changing World* (both Routledge) and has written many other books and articles on analytical psychology and Jungian psychoanalysis.

Elena Caramazza, MD and Pediatrician, is an IAAP member, AIPA preceptor, and Jungian analyst. She has published several papers and reviews concerning Jungian thought and analytical psychology and practices privately as an analyst in Rome.

Temporality, Shame, and the Problem of Evil in Jungian Psychology

An Exchange of Ideas

Murray Stein and Elena Caramazza

Routledge
Taylor & Francis Group
LONDON AND NEW YORK

First published 2021
by Routledge
2 Park Square, Milton Park, Abingdon, Oxon OX14 4RN

and by Routledge
52 Vanderbilt Avenue, New York, NY 10017

Routledge is an imprint of the Taylor & Francis Group, an informa business

British Library Cataloguing in Publication Data
A catalogue record for this book is available from the British Library

Library of Congress Cataloging-in-Publication Data
A catalog record has been requested for this book

ISBN: 978-0-367-46576-6 (hbk)
ISBN: 978-0-367-46577-3 (pbk)
ISBN: 978-1-003-02968-7 (ebk)

Typeset in Times New Roman
by Taylor & Francis Books

Contents

List of figures   ix
Acknowledgments   x
Foreword   xi
CLEMENTINA PAVONI
Premise   xvi
ELENA CARAMAZZA

1   Music for another age: Wolfgang Pauli's "The Piano
    Lesson" – Rome, April 2016   1
    MURRAY STEIN

2   Outline of a question for Murray Stein: The time
    dimensions: a comparison between Panikkar and Jung, 20
    January 2018   15
    ELENA CARAMAZZA

3   The four modalities of temporality and the problem
    of shame   19
    MURRAY STEIN

4   Reflections on Murray Stein's paper "The four modalities
    of temporality and the problem of shame": Synchronicity
    as the bridge between achronicity and chronicity   46
    ELENA CARAMAZZA

5   Erich Neumann and C.G. Jung on "the problem of evil"   56
    MURRAY STEIN

6   The problem of evil   65
ELENA CARAMAZZA

Afterword   71
FULVIA DE BENEDITTIS, SANDRA FERSURELLA AND
SILVIA PRESCIUTTINI

Appendix   85
Index   94

Figures

1.1 A diagram worked out by Jung and Pauli   4
1.2 Eric Neumann, "The Planes of Reality"   5
1.3 The centering of the personality   7
1.4 Imaginary and real numbers. Imaginary numbers (vertical),
    real numbers (horizontal)   10
3.1 Four modes of temporality   20
3.2 Times four   37
3.3 "The Ring i"   39
3.4 Times Four with the Ring i 39
3.5 Levels of temporality   40

Acknowledgments

I would like to thank first of all Murray Stein who agreed to have an exchange of ideas concerning his lecture at AIPA of Rome in April 2016, *Music for Another Era: Wolfgang Pauli's "Piano Lesson."*

My gratitude goes to my colleague and friend Clementina Pavoni for her Forward which seizes the most meaningful features of the dialogue between Murray Stein and me.

I thank my colleagues Fulvia De Benedittis, Sandra Ferzurella, and Silvia Presciuttini, family therapists, for their Afterword: my chapters in the book benefit a great deal from their clinical experience.

A special thanks to Heather Evans who helped me with advice in the preparation of the manuscript.

Paola Cascino caught the spirit of Murray Stein's writings with her translation which allowed me to fully understand his approach.

Susie Ann White deserves a special thank for faithfully interpretating in her English translation the chapters I wrote.

I would like to thank my colleagues of the board of *Studi Junghiani*, who invited Murray Stein to hold a lecture at AIPA and later on were of help in drafting the book.

Finally I would like to thank my Italian publisher Moretti&Vitali who encouraged me to conceive this book.

Last but not least my husband Mino Vianello helped me in this undertaking: without his constant encouragement, this book would not have existed.

Chapter 3 was originally published in Hinton & Willemsen (eds.), *Temporality and Shame* (Routledge, 2017), pp 214–241.

Elena Caramazza

Foreword

Clementina Pavoni

Books in the form of an epistolary dialogue, like this one, fascinate the reader and involve them in the development of the reciprocal thoughts.

Here, one enters the debate that Murray Stein and Elena Caramazza conduct on the concept of time, and on two aspects in particular: the finite time of the cosmic clock and the eternal time of the unconscious and the Self, also exploring the difficulty of experiencing these two temporal dimensions simultaneously. Then, there is the time of the reflections exchanged by Caramazza and Stein – not, I imagine, that of the traditional post, but the real time of emails sent from a computer or tablet.

As Caramazza explains in her Preface, it all began in Rome in April 2016 with Murray Stein's lecture on "The Piano Lesson" by Wolfgang Pauli, in which the great physicist undertakes an active imagination to explore the possibilities and problems of uniting the mathematical time of science and the eternal time of the psyche. The key image in the active imagination is the black and white keys of the piano, which, together, compose the various chords. This made Caramazza think of Panikkar and his concept of "tempiternity," and she told Stein how his lecture had resonated with her. Thus, this profound and intense exchange was born, which starts from the image of musical chords and continues by describing the difficulties of achieving inner harmonies, due to the fact that we all exist in the two kinds of time. Their dialogue considers the problems that arise when these harmonies are blocked or disrupted in life by traumatic experiences, and external time is blocked through endless repetition; or when, by contrast, there is a total shift to the harmony between matter and psyche, triggered by the creative act of discovering meaning and of the "surprising" phenomenon of synchronicity.

Murray Stein says:

What synchronicity introduces into the discussion of chance events is "meaning," by which I designate, following Jung, a realization that derives from and points to something transcendent, spiritual, coming from a source beyond any figures featured in the event. Additionally, synchronicity derives from a source that is autonomous and creative, which lies beyond both psyche and matter. Jung speaks of synchronicities as "acts of creation in time."

To which Caramazza replies:

I also think that the creative act goes way beyond the decision or choice made by the Ego, which are linked to the discriminating faculty of the intellect, since it springs from a source that draws on the depths of the Self, where the Self, in the Jungian sense, is not only a dimension of the individual, but also embraces others and, indeed, the entire cosmos. When hands think and words evoke, we may suppose that they are telling a story about the Self.

The value of this book lies in the harmony of its reflections as notes of a composition for four hands.

Here, I cannot help thinking of that particular form of timelessness that exists in certain paintings, which comes alive every time we look at them, taking us into another dimension. Iconic images whose meaning is expressed through the forms and sounds they conjure, activating our feelings and bringing us alive. Like Vermeer's *Milkmaid*, which in Wisława Szymborska's poem transports us into the dimension of the eternal.

So long as that woman from the Rijksmuseum
In painted quiet and concentration
Keeps pouring milk day after day
From the pitcher to the bowl
The World hasn't earned
The world's end.

In the poem the milkmaid is evoked as an icon, which through a fixed gesture, repeated ad infinitum, enters the temporal dimension that Murray Stein calls *achronicity*: "achronicity is myth's modality of temporality ... Iconic constancy is the most characteristic element in the description of myths."

The World cannot end because in this timeless time there is no beginning and no end. It is the time of "tempiternity," which – as

Caramazza explains through a metaphor coined by Panikkar – is not the time of a drop of water that disappears in the sea, but of the drop that becomes part of its waters.

Basing themselves on the conceptual schema of the four modalities of temporality (achronicity-chronicity, syncronicity-dyschronicity) theorized by Stein, the two authors interestingly interpret – with important implications for clinical psychology – crucial themes that are not always strictly psychological, such as "the challenging problem of evil" (Caramazza) and, consequently, the difficulty of passing through and embracing the Shadow and of accepting one's own destiny, all of which are considered in relation to the "qualities" of time as differentiated in the schema. Moreover, chronicity, or measurable time, and memory begin precisely at the point where the two axes indicating the four modalities of time intersect. And with memory, comes a sense of our own finiteness. The Bible teaches that guilt and shame, which overlap, came into being when Adam and Eve were banished from the Garden of Eden. Entering the dimension of time implies a "knowledge" of evil – a world that was wholly good would be a static world, without time or active negative drive and without memory, existing in a never-ending, absolute present.

We have all experienced achronicity in the womb, from which, however, we are forcibly expelled, and in the syntonic relationship between mother and infant – when this happy situation exists. Here, it is a question of fate. It depends on where our destiny has taken us, and also on how we have been, or are, able to mend the fractures, at times inevitable and at others traumatic, caused by our experiences of syntony, the achronistic time of synchronicity. In other words, that timeless time (achronicity) – found in the Bible and the syntony of the mother-infant relationship – when, as Stein writes, there exists a "complete and smooth harmony between supply and demand, between inner need and outer fulfillment, between psyche and world."

In everyone's life there are ecstatic moments of absolute harmony with the emotive world of the psyche and the great world of nature; moments in which there are no barriers or differences between self and the world of things, and we feel part of an embracing, timeless whole. They are those moments – but only moments – that gradually disappear as we find ourselves in common time again, as if waking from a spell. Exactly as Montale describes in the following poem:

> To pass noon, pale and thoughtful,
> Near a hot orchard wall …

> To observe through the leaves the heartbeat
> Faraway of flakes of sea ...
> To go into the sun that dazzles
> To feel with sad wonder
> How all life and its labour
> In this going on is a wall
> That has on top sharp shards of bottles.

The last verse brings us back to reality, to the here and now, after time has been suspended at noon, when the sun was at its zenith before gradually descending to the horizon.

The "sharp shards of bottles" are not the same for everyone: injustice is at work in things and human beings. Walls are not all the same. Trauma can block time in dyschronicity. Thus, we might say that dyschronistic time is the time of a trauma that does not pass, one that is not thinkable – hence not conscious – and still present and active. The time of oblivion and not of memory. Or the time of trauma that is repeated endlessly, unconsciously, which makes it incomprehensible. A *mechanism* – as it is insightfully described by an analysand quoted by Caramazza. A time that restores actions, feelings, and memories from oblivion, becoming a coercive, repetitive action that is always the same but unconscious, precisely because memories are placed in non-experienced, *achronistic* time, as in Stein's schema. It is the time of a trauma that is suffered but not consciously thought of.

It is not a question of repressing and obliviating the traumatic event, but of obliterating it, like a postage stamp, so that it becomes unusable. As if it had not happened and no longer existed. Thus the past does not pass and exists in an eternal present. Without life. Without memory.

> A hopeless love, killed like the Nevers love. Therefore already relegated to oblivion. Therefore eternal. [Protected by oblivion itself.][1]

This is how Marguerite Duras describes the temporal dimension of the trauma experienced by the female protagonist of *Hiroshima mon amour*. A trauma consigned to the time of dyschronicity, to oblivion that renders it eternal, present in the thoughts of the dream:

> Nevers is the city in the world, and even the thing in the world, I dream about most often at night. And at the same time it's the thing I think about the least.[2]

In psychoanalytic work, which is carried out in a protected room and, to some extent, outside the time of *chronicity*, but where each word, each gesture, and each look, God willing, can trigger a flash of understanding, one experiences – though certainly not always – brief moments of synchronistic time. *Noontide* moments that mend the fractures in the timeline and restore an affective memory of our own past. Thus life can flow smoothly along the linear path of chronistic time and encounter synchronistic moments, which are bearers of meaning – a concept expressed by Caramazza with regard to one of her childhood memories, and taken up by Stein to explore the possibility of recovering and reconciling the fractures of experience.

As Murray Stein and Elena Caramazza develop their ideas, they find themselves confronting the nature and cause of evil. Two narratives are compared: that of the biblical myth, mentioned above, and that of the Indian myth of Prajapati. Both myths make reference to guilt, but in the biblical story it stems from Adam and Eve's act of disobedience, while in the Indian narrative it derives from the god Prajapati, who creates the world to escape from his solitude, and in so doing also creates darkness. Here it is not humanity, represented by the two progenitors, who foregoes the paradisiacal fullness of Being, that is a world without evil, out of guilt, but the god himself who eludes the Absolute, with humanity representing the consequence of "a kind of affront or challenge to the absolute" made by Prajapati.

In both narratives, guilt lies at the origin of the world as we know it, meaning that evil, which generates guilt, is inherent in our existence.

Milan, May 2019

Notes

1 M. Duras (1960), *Hiroshima mon amour* (trans. Richard Seaver), Grove Press, New York 1961.
2 Ibid.

Premise

Elena Caramazza

In April 2016, at the AIPA Center in Rome, I attended Murray Stein's lecture *Music for Another Era – Wolfgang Pauli's "Piano Lesson."* As a reaction, I wrote this comment and sent it to him.

As Murray Stein tells it, Pauli, after entering in contact with Jung, worried about the difference between Quantum Physics and Psychoanalysis and was trying to combine them in an unified theory. If Science supplies the words for an explanation of the world, Psychoanalysis supplies the meaning of these words, but how to conciliate them in a common language? Pauli's answer is "thanks to the piano music," where you need to have recourse to black and white keys. It is from the harmony stemming from piano music that causality and synchronicity would match in an unique theory.

Murray Stein interprets and completes Pauli's symbolic image by suggesting that the white keys represent the positivistic and mathematical approach to describe and analyze the relation between material objects from a non-psychological perspective, since the psyche is as much as possible excluded from the observation field, while the black keys represent the meaning, the qualitative aspect of reality which is the object of life experience. When both keys are played, one hears the music of an unified world where empirical facts, mathematical laws, and meaning merge together and result in harmony. Piano music in which both keys are involved gives us the feeling of living in a world where science and meaning, endowed with an infinite echo in the depth of our psyche, concur to create a feeling of completeness and harmony of our existence in relationship with the whole reality.

This correspondence with Murray Stein stems from the fact that he replied to a comment that I sent him few days afterwards in which, on the topic of causality and synchronicity, I referred to Raimon Panikkar's conception of "tempiternity" in which time and eternity are inextricably fused, and eternity is seen as "time's non-temporal root."

An exchange of ideas on these issues followed that led to a reflection on our experience of time as framework of emotions like shame and the unfathomable mystery of Evil.

Chapter 1

Music for another age

Wolfgang Pauli's "The Piano Lesson" – Rome, April 2016

Murray Stein

I was delighted to accept your surprising invitation to continue the reflection on synchronicity that I began in the essay, "Synchronizing Time and Eternity," which you have kindly translated into Italian and published in your journal, *Studi Junghiani*. In this lecture, I will again turn to Wolfgang Pauli's "The Piano Lesson" and take the view that this work was an active imagination that had a profound transformative effect on the author. It seems to me, also, that this essay in active imagination and creative thinking by Pauli, which he dedicated to Dr. von Franz, his analyst, offers us a novel and highly suggestive entry point into exploring the question of what it means to live in consciousness of the interpenetration and interplay of causality and synchronicity in the here and now. In the language of Pauli's essay, this is "piano music," or what Herbert van Erkelens (2002, p. 120) has proposed to call "symphonicity." Taking a cue from Beethoven's comment about his Opus 59 Quartets, that they were written not for the audience in 1806 but for a later age (cited in Dusinberre 2016, p. 6), I am titling this lecture "Music for a Later Age." I consider Pauli's proposal for a concept that unifies quantum physics and depth psychology, i.e., causality and synchronicity, time and the timeless, to be something still for the future. It is my conviction that we still have a long way to go before we have integrated the message in this profound proposal for a *Weltanschauung* that unifies science and spirituality.

Thank you very much for the invitation to share these reflections with you.

The problem of synchronicity

Nearly everyone I ask about it can report a synchronistic experience, and many people feel that such experiences have even changed the very course of their lives. They may not have a theory to explain it, but they know what I mean when I speak of "meaningful coincidences." Meaningful coincidences have been known and recorded since time immemorial. During religious and mythological ages, they were seen as divine interventions, as messages from the gods, or as blessings, or sometimes as curses. Since the European Enlightenment and the enshrinement of the Goddess Reason, however, moderns have dismissed such coincidences as sheer chance events and devoid of objective meaning. What meaning can be assigned to them is purely subjective and the product of wishful thinking, superstition, paranoia, or fear. It remained for Jung to bring back the notion of objective meaning and to speak of "acts of creation in time" (Jung 1952/1969, par. 965) thus disrupting the modern consensus that causality, chance, and the iron laws of nature leave nothing more to be said about the course of personal and collective life.

Wolfgang Pauli (1900–1958) worked deeply, intensely, and over a long period of time with Jung on the problem of synchronicity and its implications for modernity. In fact, Jung's major conversation partner on this subject of meaningful coincidence was without any doubt the mathematical genius and Nobel Prize winning physicist, Wolfgang Pauli. To this conversation Pauli brought his acute thinking, famous for its sharp-edged ferocity in arguments with his scientific colleagues. He also contributed something to which Jung was totally tone deaf, the language of mathematics. Pauli had impressed even Einstein when as a youth of eighteen he wrote a detailed review of his paper on the theory of relativity and its mathematical equations. Both men belonged to that elite group of scientists who revolutionized the field of theoretical physics and laid the groundwork for quantum theory and modern cosmology. This was Jung's impressively substantial conversation partner as he struggled to formulate his theory of synchronicity.

Science in the positivistic sense that it was practiced and taught in the universities was not enough for Pauli. He was a seeker after meaning and wholeness, and he suffered from a severe split in his personality between conscious and unconscious forces. For this latter condition, he sought help in 1933 from the famous psychoanalyst C.G. Jung, a fellow professor at the ETH in Zurich. From the beginning of his analysis, he recorded his dreams faithfully and sought deeper meaning in life than science and rationality had to offer. From his dreams and waking visions as recorded during his early analysis and Jung's interpretation of them in *Psychology and Alchemy*, Pt. II (Jung 1968), one could even say Pauli was a mystic in disguise as a scientist, and very well disguised indeed to the outside world. This is certainly not to take away anything from his brilliance as a mathematician and a scientific thinker.

"The Piano Lesson," composed in the fall of 1953 and so only a few short years before his death in 1958, makes clear Pauli's continuing dedicated search for a way to combine his scientific and psychological commitments. Even so late in his professional life and after twenty years of contact with Jung, he was suffering from the problem of resolving the differences between what he calls "the two schools," quantum physics and depth psychology, and struggling with the question of how to bring them together into a single unified theory. This was at the heart of his discussions with Jung as we can see in the correspondence (Meier 2001), and it is the burden of "The Piano Lesson." As Pauli puts it in this work, science offers "words" of explanation and psychology offers the "meaning" of those words, but how can he combine them into a single language? The symbolic answer is "piano music," played with both white and black keys. Causality and synchronicity must be married into a single theory.

As Jung and Pauli worked ever more deeply into the interface between quantum physics and depth psychology, they wrestled with the phenomenon of synchronicity and its implications. For science, the psyche and the material world are strictly separated domains. Humans can study the material world and discover its laws, but they are not fundamentally entangled with it. In fact, scientists do everything they can to remove the human factor, i.e., projections, personal and cultural bias, etc. They want to discover the objective laws of nature. Once these laws become known, they can be used to make predictions, to create new technologies, and generally to bring nature under greater human control through manipulation. Synchronicity, however, brings the two domains, psyche and matter, together, but not through intentional ego action. As generally defined, a synchronistic event is, as Atmanspacher and Fach summarize, "a coincidence phenomenon in which ordinarily unconnected mental and physical states are experienced as connected" (Atmanspacher and Fach 2016, p. 79) and I would add: as *meaningful*. Meaning is an essential feature of synchronicity. The theory of synchronicity is the contribution of psychology to science, but it is not an easy one to digest and integrate. The psyche is indeed entangled with the material world, and this entanglement brings meaning and creativity into play in both domains, but it remained to be worked out how this would look in life as lived and conceived as a whole.

If the factor of synchronicity in a sense transcends the factor of causality, it does not abolish it. Relating these two dimensions and bringing them together into a single unified field theory became the great challenge facing Jung and Pauli. It is comparable to bringing the East and the West into a unified world picture on the one hand, and bringing consciousness and the unconscious together in the realm of psyche on the other. The systems in both cases are incommensurate, as Jung states clearly in a letter to Pauli (Meier 2001, p. 61), and yet they must be brought into a unified whole if a full picture of reality, whether psychic or cosmic, is to be drawn. Similarly, when one consults the *I Ching* with a Western-trained scientific mind, the two incommensurate systems are brought into play, as Jung demonstrates in his brilliant "Foreword to the *I Ching*" (Jung 1950/1969, 964–1018). In the correspondence between Jung and Pauli, one finds various proposals for how to diagram a world picture that would include both causality and synchronicity (Meier 2001, pp. 56–61). Jung published their final version in his essay, "Synchronicity: An Acausal Connecting Principle" (Jung 1952/1969, par. 963).

What synchronicity introduces into the discussion of chance events is "meaning," by which I designate, following Jung, a realization that derives from and points to something transcendent, spiritual, coming from a source beyond any figures featured in the event. Additionally, synchronicity derives from a source that is autonomous and creative, which lies beyond both psyche and matter. Jung speaks of synchronicities as "acts of creation in time" (Jung 1952/1969, par. 965). It is these three features of synchronicity – the unity of psyche and world, transcendent meaning, and creativity – that challenged the scientific world picture in Jung's time and does so still also in ours. Synchronicity theory disrupts our modern way of thinking to such a degree that a scientist like Pauli was disturbed to the core of his being by it. In "The Piano Lesson" he tries to find a solution to the question of how these two principles – lawful causality on the one hand, and synchronicity on the other – can be brought together in a unified theory. The further question is: how is this experienced?

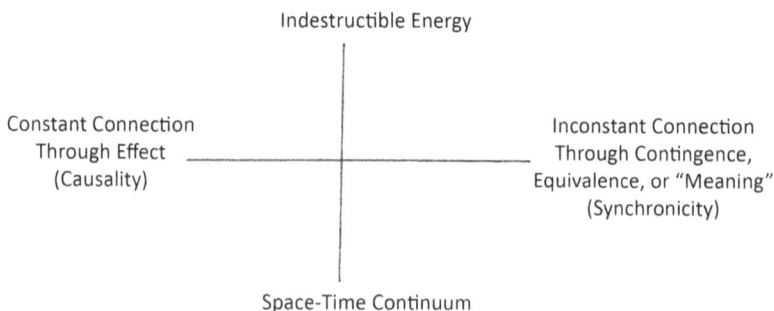

Indestructible Energy

Constant Connection
Through Effect
(Causality)

Inconstant Connection
Through Contingence,
Equivalence, or "Meaning"
(Synchronicity)

Space-Time Continuum

Figure 1.1 A diagram worked out by Jung and Pauli

The Piano Lesson as active imagination

To understand how Pauli approaches this problem – and perhaps suc-
ceeds in solving it for himself, as we shall see – we need to begin by
looking at the method he uses for engaging it, i.e., active imagination.
Jung developed active imagination as a method in order to create what
he called a transcendent function, that is, a bridge or connection
between ego-consciousness and the unconscious. When successful, active
imagination introduces a disruption in normal ego-consciousness in
such a way that it is able to step beyond its usual boundaries and
enter into a dialogue with unconscious figures and images. As a result,
the ego moves into contact with what Erich Neumann called the
archetypal field and the self-field.

Let me take a moment to explain this drawing (Figure 1.2), which
Neumann includes in his Eranos paper, "The Psyche and the Transformation of the Reality Planes" (Neumann 1952/1989, pp. 3–62). The
diagram represents three fields of knowledge: an ego field, an archetypal
field, and a self-field. There are also three stages, or states, of consciousness, which move in the diagram from left to right: a) Constellation of Consciousness, b) Constellation of the Archetypal Field
(Embeddedness), and c) Centering of the Personality. The three stages
show different levels of relationship among the fields below the ego
level and differing degrees of separation between psyche and world
above the ego field. As the stages move from left to right, the three fields
come closer – you see the bottom levels rising upward. At the top, there
are three degrees of separation between psyche and world, and moving

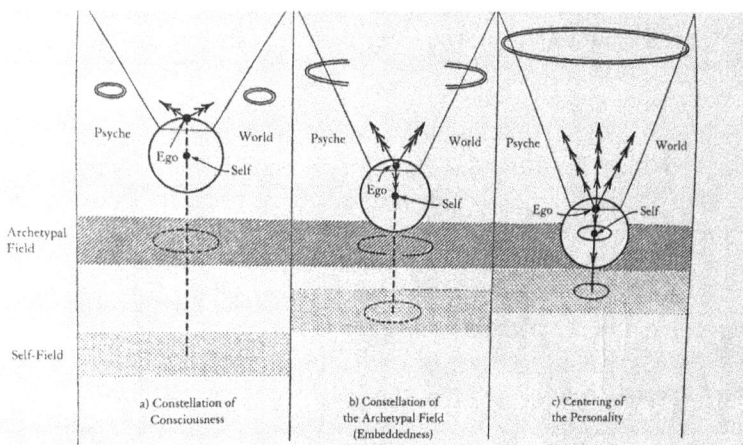

Figure 1.2 Eric Neumann, "The Planes of Reality"

from left to right we see this distance closing. Moving from left to right, the bottom rises and the top closes as the state of consciousness achieves what Neumann calls "centering of the personality." Our interest is in the movement toward awareness of *unus mundus*, which unites psyche and world through bringing causality and synchronicity together.

The stage on the far left represents modern consciousness, which divides awareness between inner subjective and outer objective spaces, and between conscious and unconscious within the inner realm. There is no connection between them. On an everyday level, most of us live in the state of awareness on the left. Common sense, education, and modern secular attitudes lend their weight to dividing the world and psyche in this way. Occasionally, we may sense ourselves in the middle stage, when material from the archetypal field impinges on our awareness, as in active imagination. And once in a while, perhaps, we find ourselves in the state of unified consciousness represented on the right where all the levels and divided worlds unite.

Once the ego is in closer contact with these fields, the gap between psyche and matter begins to close and a sense of *unus mundus*, i.e., a unified world, emerges. Neumann explains this in detail in a later Eranos paper, "The Experience of the Unitary Reality" (Neumann 1952/1989, pp. 63–130). This is precisely what we see happening in Pauli's "Piano Lesson":

> I have the impression that the white keys are like the words and the black keys are like the meaning. At times the words are sad and the meaning joyful, then again it is just the other way round. Here, with you, it is no longer as in the two schools which gave me so much trouble: I can always see that there is only *one* piano.
>
> (Pauli 1954–2002, p. 126)

In this moment, Pauli reaches a position in which the two schools combine their contributions and a single piece of music is heard.

"The Piano Lesson" begins with a sudden reversal of time, or what we might call a regression, to a period in Pauli's life when he was a teenager. In his old home back in Vienna, he finds himself in the presence of an impressive older woman, who is identified as the piano teacher. He is here to take a lesson. As we move through the story, three figures emerge as the main characters: Pauli himself, the female figure or anima who takes a couple of forms, and the Master, or Self-figure. Both the female figures and the Master have a history in Pauli's earlier dreams and active imaginations, which I will not detail here (see Van Erkelens and Wiegel 2002, pp. 135–141). "The Piano Lesson" becomes a story of

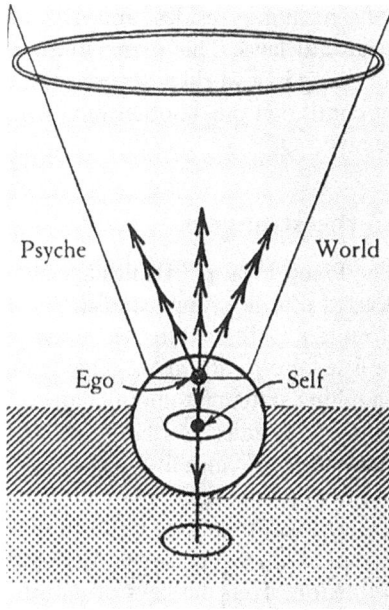

Figure 1.3 The centering of the personality

establishing solid relations among these three figures, and this is precisely what occurs in Neumann's third stage of consciousness.

The anima figure, i.e., the piano teacher, presents the archetypal field, and the Master, i.e., the Self-figure, presents the Self-field. When they are all brought together, Pauli finds that there is no longer any conflict between the "two schools" and piano playing on both white and black keys becomes a possibility. What does this mean?

The white keys represent the school of positivistic science and mathematics, a language for describing and investigating the relations among material objects from a non-psychic standpoint. The psyche is excluded as much as possible from the field. The black keys represent the language of meaning, the qualitative rather than the quantitative side of experienced reality. Here psyche is the essential component in the investigation. When the two are brought together and music is played with both black and white keys, one hears the music of a unified world where empirical fact and mathematical law and meaning all sound together. Causality and synchronicity unite in a single field. The white keys do not exclude the black keys, as one finds in the science departments of the universities as Pauli says; nor do the black keys exclude the white keys as one might find in the theological schools and religions where only meaning resides and tries to dominate over empirical fact and natural laws. This piano music combines both, so one gets the sense of living in a world where science and meaning come together and do not contradict one another but rather each contributes some notes to the whole.

Pauli's lecture to the strangers

In the course of "The Piano Lesson," Pauli's age changes several times. First he slides backward into his youth, and then he comes forward to his present age. Now, and still within the active imagination, he is called upon to give a lecture to strangers. This comes about suddenly when Pauli makes a telling statement about chance. Generally, the idea that nature operates by fixed rules and laws dominates the thinking of scientists. The absolute rule of causality is the result. In the world of quantum physics, however, the rigid laws of nature seem to be suspended, and probability takes their place. But probability is not secure, and blind chance can easily bring about disruptive surprises. This opens the doors to freedom from the laws of nature, but it does not in any way include the element of meaning. Chance is blind and has no purpose. At this point in the active imagination, Pauli says: "chance is always fluctuating, but sometimes it fluctuates systematically" (Pauli 1954–2002, p. 127). It is these systematic fluctuations that open the door to possible meaning.

Here an abrupt change occurs in the active imagination, and Pauli is instructed by the Master to give a lecture to a throng of strangers who appear outside the window. Pauli is now his present age, and speaks as a professor. This will be the inauguration of his new vocational mission, to occupy the chair of unified quantum physics and depth psychology. His lecture is on biology, however, and he argues that evolution is based on two principles: adaptation to environments and chance mutations. The chance mutations can be shown to follow a pattern of systematic fluctuations such that a line of development occurs from simple organisms eventually to the human being and the human psyche, an organism that is capable of advanced forms of consciousness. This is a development in nature that shows underlying meaningful coincidence all along the way. Pauli points out that mutations often occur before they demonstrate their importance for adaptation to environment, hence they are not responses to environmental pressures but rather originate elsewhere in some source of underlying creativity.

This anomaly in the pattern of mutations brings into play the notion that creativity resides in a location within reality that implies meaning and purpose. Creativity has purpose, even if this cannot be seen in the moment of its appearance in material reality. In other words, synchronicity takes place in nature and in history apart from humankind and also when humans are not around to recognize it. This is a broader definition of synchronicity than Jung started with, namely the meaningful coincidence between psyche and matter. The natural world in and of itself also participates in the principle of synchronicity. Synchronicity happens, then causality follows, and further developments show lawful pathways. The two principles work together. This is piano playing, or what van Erkelens called symphonicity.

After Pauli's lecture to the strangers, the anima figure cries out: "Ich glaube, du hast mir ein Kind gemacht" (Pauli 1954/1995, p. 327; "I think you have given me a child"). Apparently his lecture has brought about a *coniunctio* and generated an offspring that represents the union of ego and anima, i.e., a "third thing," or unified position. This is a further symbolic expression of union, like the piano playing that unites the action of both black and white keys to produce music.

"The Ring *i*"

"The Piano Lesson" concludes with a highly symbolic scene in which the anima figure removes a ring from her finger, which Pauli had not noticed until now. The ring symbolizes the union between Pauli and the woman who has just born him a child, and it is designated as "the ring *i*" (Pauli 1954–2002, p. 134).

The symbol "*i*" speaks in the language of mathematics. It is an "imaginary unit" that opens up new dimensions within mathematical fields.

With this symbol, "complex numbers" can be created, which combine real and imaginary numbers. The symbol *i* is a sort of magical unifier of opposites, in alchemical terms a Mercurius figure. "The *i* makes the void and the unit into a couple," Pauli says to the woman (Pauli 1954–2002, p. 134). This is a union of unconscious (the void) and ego-consciousness (the unit). To which she replies: "It makes the instinctive or impulsive, the intellectual or rational, the spiritual or supernatural … into a unified or monadic whole that the numbers without the *i* cannot represent" (p. 134). In other words, it unifies all levels of being, material, psychological/mental, and spiritual. Here it is presented in the form of a very special kind of wedding ring: "It is the marriage and at the same time the realm of the middle, which you can never reach alone but only in pairs" (p. 134). This states that the goal of arriving at and living permanently in the realms of wholeness – the

$$Im$$

$$z = x + iy$$

$$\overline{z} = x - iy$$

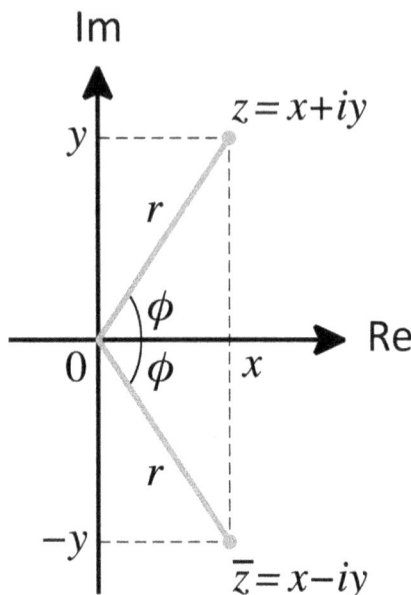

Figure 1.4 Imaginary and real numbers. Imaginary numbers (vertical), real numbers (horizontal)

unified world – can be accomplished only if the two schools, the two languages, ego-consciousness and the archetypal unconscious, walk on this path together as a couple. The "ring *i*" is the symbol of their irrational and eternal bond, now consummated.

This consummation is then impressively affirmed by "the voice of the Master," who "speaks, transformed, from the center of the ring to the lady: 'Remain compassionate'" (Pauli 1954–2002, p. 134).[1] This is a reference to the closing stanzas of Goethe's *Faust*, where Doctor Marianus speaks the lines:

> Jungfrau, Mutter, Königin,
> Göttin, bleibe gnädig!
> [Virgin, Mother, Queen,
> Goddess, remain compassionate.]

It is a prayer for the future and a blessing for the union between Pauli and the woman who has offered him "the ring *i*" and born a child with him. The eternal feminine is invoked and elevated to her highest and most complete status. In the context of "The Piano

Lesson," this means that the woman figure is also healed and transformed, and she is now freed to assume an intimate and permanent relationship with the protagonist. Their union is complete and blessed.

The lysis of the story

This would be the end of a fairy tale, but it is not quite the end of "The Piano Lesson." After hearing the blessing from the Master, Pauli suddenly finds himself out of the framework of the fantasy and back in normal time and space, i.e., no longer in the ego-archetypal-self constellation as described by Neumann as the third stage, but rather back to the first. In other words, the active imagination is over, and the normal state of ego-consciousness returns. Now Pauli is again wearing his professorial coat and tie and goes about his business. As he walks away, he hears the woman at the piano. She plays a C-major chord of four notes C E G C. This has been compared to a quaternity symbol and to the famous saying of the alchemist Marie Prophetessa: "Out of the one comes the two; out of the two comes the three; and out of the three comes the one as the fourth" (Atmanspacher et al. 1995, p. 340). This affirmative major chord signals a sense of completion and a successful culmination of this lesson at the piano, and because Pauli can still hear her play, it means, in my opinion, that their relationship remains alive even though they are now apart and he can only hear the melodies at a distance. A significant transformation has taken place within his psychic matrix.

An open question

A question remains, however, about how to understand this ending. It is normal to return to one's usual ego-consciousness and identity following an intense active imagination. However, some commentators, like Herbert Van Erkelens (Van Erkelens and Wiegel 2002, p. 140) and M.-L. von Franz (2002, pp. 142–8), have taken this ending to mean that Pauli abandoned the project. Although he has promised to return to the home of the piano teacher and has been given a new vocation to teach about the harmonious interface of physics and psychology, he reneges on his promises. He never returns, he never carries this purposeful mission into the world of his profession, and he simply closes the lesson and forgets about it. This is their harsh judgment, but I do not find it entirely persuasive.

It seems to me that the marriage has effectively taken place, and on an inner level Pauli has forged a permanent and transformative bond with the anima. This is meant for his own private purposes, however, and not for the outer world of his professional or social life. On the outer level, this inner marriage may have been reflected in some subtle ways in his behavior and relationships, but it was not made explicit in his lectures or writings afterwards. It was a private mystical experience that was meant for him alone, although he shared it with his analyst and indeed dedicated it to her, but otherwise he kept it private as a carefully guarded secret. My intuition tells me that he continued to play the piano for himself, that he continued to hear the music of causality and synchronicity combined throughout the remainder of his life. This would mean that he did indeed continue to see the various events of life, from the largest to smallest, as meaningful, and that he kept a watchful eye on the lookout for new acts of creation in time.

But perhaps this was music for a future age, and that age would be ours. It is then left for us to nurture and raise the child born to Pauli and the Lady in "The Piano Lesson." One might take this beginning further, as Jung and Pauli (1952/1955) suggested, and Neumann (1958/1989) and von Franz (1992) did in their own time. More recently, Atmanspacher and Fach (2013) have proposed a structural-phenomenological typology of mind-matter correlations. I will not go further into this fruitful development here, but rather only confirm that this work is being done presently by a variety of people and at a sophisticated intellectual level. Clinical applications of this correlation theory have been taken up by Joseph Cambray (2009), Angela Connolly (2015), and Yvonne Smith Klitsner (2015).

Conclusion

The other day in Zurich I saw a sign in front of a sweets shop: "A Day without Chocolate is like Champagne without Bubbles." Yes, I thought: that would be "flat." Now it occurs to me that a world ruled by causality alone and without synchronicity would be the same: A World without Synchronicity is like Champagne without Bubbles – "flat." Imagine a life without meaningful coincidence that turns you in an entirely new direction; a world in which everything is completely and rigidly predicable; a world without creativity and surprise, without disruption, without the beautiful possibility of a chance encounter with a stranger that turns out to be transformative for your life. This would indeed be champagne without bubbles.

Thank goodness we do not live in such a world.

Some months after our correspondence began, Murray Stein sent me a theatre version he did of Wolfgang Paul's The Piano Lesson. The text is reproduced in the Appendix.

Note

1 Author's substitution of "compassionate" for "merciful."

Bibliography

Atmanspacher, H. and Fach, W. (2013). A Structural-Phenomenological Typology of Mind-Matter Correlations. *Journal of Analytical Psychology* 58/2, 219–244.

Atmanspacher, H. and Fach, W. (2016). Synchronistic Mind-Matter Correlations in Therapeutic Practice. *Journal of Analytical Psychology* 61/1, 79.

Cambray, J. (2009). *Synchronicity: Nature and Psyche in an Interconnected Universe*. College Station: Texas A&M University Press.

Connolly, A. (2015). Bridging the Reductive and the Synthetic: Some Reflections on the Clinical Implications of Synchronicity. *Journal of Analytical Psychology* 60/2, 159–178.

Dusinberre, E. (2016). *Beethoven for a Later Age*. London: Faber & Faber.

Jung, C.G. (1950/1969). Foreword to the I Ching. *Collected Works*, vol. 11. Princeton, NJ: Princeton University Press.

Jung, C.G. (1952/1969). Synchronizität als ein Prinzip akusaler Zusammenhänge, Synchronicity: An Acausal Connecting Principle. *Collected Works*, vol. 8. Princeton, NJ: Princeton University Press.

Jung, C.G. (1968). Psychology and Alchemy. *Collected Works*, vol. 12. Princeton, NJ: Princeton University Press.

Jung, C.G. (1976). Sincronicità come principio di nessi a-causali. In *Opere*, vol. VIII, *La dinamica dell'inconscio*. Torino: Boringhieri.

Jung, C.G. and Pauli, W. (1952/1955). *The Interpretation of Nature and the Psyche*. New York: Pantheon Books.

Klitsner, Y.S. (2015). Synchronicity, Intentionality, and Archetypal Meaning Therapy. *Jung Journal* 9/4, 26–37.

Meier, C.A. (ed.) (2001). *Atom and Archetype: The Pauli/Jung Letters 1932–1958*. Princeton, NJ: Princeton University Press.

Neumann, E. (1952/1989). The Psyche and the Transformation of the Reality Planes, A Metapsychological Essay. In *The Place of Creation*. Princeton, NJ: Princeton University Press, pp. 3–62.

Neumann, E. (1958/1989). The Experience of the Unitary Reality. In *The Place of Creation*, Princeton, NJ: Princeton University Press, pp. 63–130.

Pauli, W. (1954/1995). Die Klavierstunde. Eine active Phantasie über das Unbewusste. In *Der Pauli-Jung Dialog und seine Beteuteng für die modern*

Wissenchaft (eds. H. Armanspacher, H. Primas, E. Wertenschlang-Birkhäuser). Berlin: Springer.

Pauli, W. (1954–2002). The Piano Lesson, *Harvest* 48/2, 122–134.

Van Erkelens, H. (2002). Introduction to The Piano Lesson. *Harvest* 48/2, 120.

Van Erkelens, H. and Wiegel, F.W. (2002). Commentary on The Piano Lesson. *Harvest* 48/2, 135–141.

Von Franz, M.-L. (1992). *Psyche and Matter*. Boston and London: Shambhala.

Von Franz, M.-L. (2002). In interview with Herbert van Erkelens. *Harvest* 48/2, 142–148.

Chapter 2

Outline of a question for Murray Stein

The time dimensions: a comparison between Panikkar and Jung, 20 January 2018

Elena Caramazza

I am wondering if your eloquent metaphor of the "piano lesson," which involves a duet between black and white keys, and of the "symphony of life" that unfolds from the inextricably interwoven dimensions of causality and synchronicity, might not be echoed in Raimon Panikkar's thought, some essential points of which I will set forth here. One of Panikkar's great intuitions was the indissoluble relationship between time and eternity, for which he coined the term "tempiternity." Here eternity is not a time that is everlasting, but rather the non-temporal root of time – *kairos* in a certain sense – the time of meaning and depth, which is more qualitative than quantitative because it is neither linear nor homogeneous, and signals the emergence of the new, which is not a consequence but a beginning. I also think that the creative act goes way beyond the decision or choice made by the Ego, which are linked to the discriminating faculty of the intellect, since it springs from a source that draws on the depths of the Self, where the Self, in the Jungian sense, is not only a dimension of the individual, but also embraces others and, indeed, the entire cosmos. On the other hand, opening ourselves to the new and allowing the unknown aspect of ourselves and of reality to emerge requires the courage to step into the void, precisely because what will be born has no precedent and is not even implicit in the pure potential of being (moreover, the image we are able to conjure of the "new" is only a pale rendition of what will actually take place). At the precise moment that the creative act is performed what previously did not exist acquires a form and light. In this sense, I believe that the creative act interrupts the process of pure causality in a novel way. As Panikkar writes, human consciousness has a dimension that cannot be reduced to historical consciousness:

Reality is basically discontinuous. We create time. Time does not sustain us like a mother. It is our child. The creative moment is the only reality. History is woven from the detritus, as it were, of authentic human activity, and of any activity.

(Panikkar 1981/1984, p. 81; 1998: p. 124)

From this standpoint, I think that the creative act does not only pro-duce the "effective" dimension of reality and history, but also fosters all the possibilities of being which, although they may not necessarily become a reality, will constitute the aura, depth, and further meaning and mystery of every symbolic expression, which also includes the invisible. As Jung writes, fostering a symbolic attitude to consciousness means "putting a veil on things as they really are" (1911/1952; 1970, p. 226). Besides, for Jung "making history" implies, as it were, the capacity to be "antihistorical" since it means overcoming historical inertia, which can be likened to the driving force of the causality prin-ciple, where events are determined according to previously established premises. In this sense, we may see historical inertia as representing ancient fate, or present day emotions – which often have us in their grip – and as relentlessly driven by an implacable destiny. A destiny in the guise of Atropos, the third of the Greek Moirai, "she who cannot be dissuaded." Leaving aside the powerful and eternal legacy of Greek tragedy, which has enabled us to contemplate and penetrate the dramas of living, we might seek to reinterpret the myth of Oedipus in the light of spiritual values and psychoanalytical research which have certainly led to the intense labor of the Soul, or Psyche, and question ourselves about our subjective responsibility in shaping our destiny and also that of the world. Oedipus saves his plagued city by solving the riddle of the sphinx through reason but it is not sufficient to enable him to escape his incestuous destiny. It is precisely the desire to "un-veil" the riddle, thus reducing it to "nothing but" a riddle for children, that denies him the possibility of understanding its full meaning. To do that he would have had to decipher the unconscious drive that led him to "reunite" with his actual mother, and transform it into the aspiration to seek out a symbolic equivalent of the mother. This would have enabled him to penetrate the mystery of his origins, to refrain from taking literally the stories that he was told, and to go beyond the curse of the oracles and the violence of paternal condemnation. Only by "forgiving" his father through a creative act that would have freed him from the con-sequences of the past, that is by restoring to his father "as a gift" (at least at the level of imagined possibilities that constellate the inter-nal object) the foresight and generosity that he had lacked in the relationship with his son, would he have been able to avoid identifying with him unconsciously as a "historic" father, and symmetrically replicating his crime. Thus he would have been able to free his country and his family from the chain of vengeful acts that had bloodied previous generations, and threatened future ones. Oedipus would have had to have become blind like Tiresias to see what we cannot see with our eyes.

Kairòs is also linked to *kronos*, which can be considered the measurable dimension of time in which the sequential chain of causes and effects that mark the majority of historical events operates. Therefore, might we not see *kronos* and *kairòs* as analogous to the black and white keys of the piano, necessary for playing the melody of life?

For Panikkar eternity lies in the "here" and "now," in the intensely experienced present that pierces the flow of becoming and thus pertains to a transhistorical dimension. From this perspective, the present can be considered as the temporal dimension of eternity:

> Those moments for which we would have given our entire life, those artistic experiences that seem to be atemporal, the realms of life that open up in deep meditation, besides the peak and ecstatic experiences in the face of the mysteries of life, suffering and death could be adduced as examples of human consciousness which are irreducible to historical consciousness.
>
> (Panikkar 1981/1984, p. 19. English: p. 81)

In particular, concerning death – which definitely pertains to chronological time – Panikkar told us at a seminar: "Death does not lie in front of me but just behind me, because the more I live the more I am distancing myself from my (deadly) non-being before the time I was." He followed this with a telling metaphor:

> Let us imagine that we are like drops of water that return to the sea. If we identify with the drop of water (our strict individuality), then death is the end of everything, because the drop disappears in the sea, but if we identify with the drop's water, with its specific quality and quantity, which is unique, then that water continues to exist together with all the other waters.

He also once said to me, to comfort me following a bereavement: "Time cannot stand still in us, but we cannot stand still in time either."

Apropos of the dual dimension of time, I remember another observation that Panikkar made during one of his discourses: "How can we

think that an hour of anxiety, an hour of suffering, an hour of joy and an hour of love are all sixty minutes long?"
My colleague Clementina Pavoni had a poetic insight inspired by these notes, seeing a parallel between the final of Goethe's *Faust* and the essential moment of experiencing the present: "Then dared I hail the Moment fleeing: 'Ah, still delay, thou art too fair! The traces cannot, of my earthly being, in aeons perish ...'" Then Clementina posed the question: "Is it the transition from *Kronos* to *Kairòs* or ... the drop of water that became ocean?"
I would like to conclude these reflections by returning to Jung, who captures the crux of Panikkar's profound intuition in the following:

Life has always seemed to me like a plant that lives on its rhizome. Its true life is invisible, hidden in the rhizome. The part that appears above ground lasts only a single summer. Then it withers away – an ephemeral apparition. When we think of the unending growth and decay of life and civilizations, we cannot escape the impression of absolute nullity. Yet I have never lost a sense of something that lives and endures underneath the eternal flux. What we see is the blossom, which passes. The rhizome remains. In the end the only events in my life worth telling are those when the imperishable world irrupted into this transitory one.

(Jung 1965, p. 22)

Bibliography

Jung, C.G. (1911/1952) Symbole der Wandlung – Analyse des Vorspiels zu einer Schizophrenie, tr. It. Simboli della Trasformazione. Analisi dei Prodromi di un Caso di Schizzofrenia, in *Opere*, vol. V, *Simboli della Trasformazione*. Boringhieri, Torino (1970).
Jung, C.G. (1965) Erinnerungen, Träume, Gedanken, tr. It., *Ricordi, Sogni, Riflessioni*, Il Saggiatore, Milano. (Revised edition, English translation by Richard Winston and Clare Winston, Vintage Books, New York 1965).
Panikkar, R. (1981/1984) L'esperienza del tempo, in *Quaderni di psicoterapia infantile*, no. 10, Tempo e psicoanalisi, Borla, Città di Castello. English: *The Cosmotheandric Experience: Emerging Religious Consciousness*, Motlilal Banarsidas Publishers, Delhi (1998).

Chapter 3

The four modalities of temporality and the problem of shame

Murray Stein

The psychological connection between temporality and shame is not a simple matter, to say the least, especially when one takes the unconscious into account. First of all, the topic of temporality is complex, and the link to shame is therefore also more than a simple registering and remembering of shameful things done present and past. Hinton cites Serres as speaking of temporality as a "folded and crumpled handkerchief" (Hinton 2015, p. 365). In this handkerchief, we inevitably find the stains of shame. How do they get there? And can they be ameliorated or even removed? If not, what is their purpose for individuation?

In this chapter, I would like to unfold and iron out this crumpled piece of fabric somewhat and try to look at the threads that go into its construction and see how and when shame enters into its weave and possibly how the problem of shame may be integrated into conscious life through an experience of the self. Is there a final, shameless state that can be achieved? Is shame like a "symptom" that is to be "transcended"? Humility, accepting the clod of earth that one is, seems to me a never ending project. And … does shame have a function or "purpose" in the development of consciousness?

Four modalities of temporality

What is time? Yiassemides begins her study of time and timelessness with the sentence: "Time is an extremely obscure concept," and quotes the Mad Hatter from Lewis Carroll's *Alice's Adventures in Wonderland*: "If you knew Time as well as I do … you wouldn't talk about … *it. It's him*" (Yiassemides 2014, p. xiii). Already we have two metaphors for time: handkerchief and Father Time. Others could be added, such as the great archetypal images of river (or snake), procession (or train),

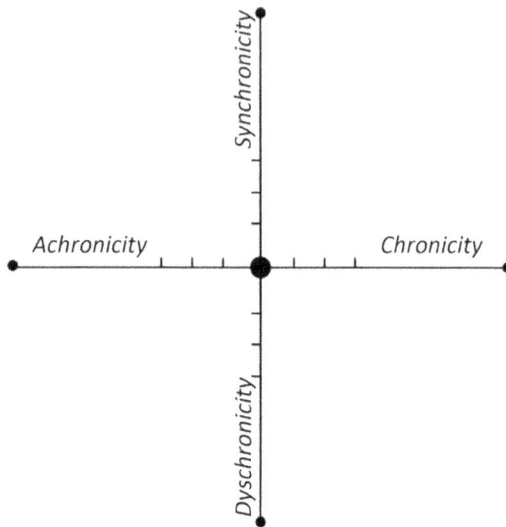

Figure 3.1 Four modes of temporality

and wheel (von Franz 1992, p. 136). Each metaphor offers a perspective on the human experience of temporality.

My approach will be more analytical and abstract, however, and will not attempt to answer the question of what time is essentially but rather to suggest that four basic modalities of temporality play a role in human consciousness in various ways and at different stages of life: achronicity, chronicity, synchronicity, and dyschronicity.[1] For purposes of this discussion, I will arrange them into two polarity pairs as shown in Figure 3.1.

The horizontal axis indicates temporality on a scale from absence to presence of the sense of chronological time. The vertical axis indicates parallel and divergent time lines that exist in real time and may fall together in consciousness. All share the term "chronicity," from the Greek word "chronos," meaning "time."

Definitions

The simplest and closest to everyday common sense of the four modes of psychological temporality is "chronicity," which indicates the normal sense of a past-present-future continuum in the waking state once a person has acquired a sense of real time and continuity of memory. Temporality as chronicity is the conscious state of awareness of the regular movement of objects like the sun and the hands of a clock in the world around us. Von Franz quotes Macrobius: "Insofar as time is a fixed measure, it is derived from the revolutions of the sky. Time begins there, and from this is believed to have been born Kronos who is Chronos. This Kronos-Saturn is the creator of time" (Von Franz 1992, p. 74). From time immemorial, humans have observed and recorded the changing seasons, the movement of the stars in the night sky, the moving slant of light that falls on a sundial, and the changes that occur in the body as the years pass by. Using this chronistic modality of temporality, it is possible to construct a personal narrative based on a time frame with specific dates and related contexts, which may resemble a piece of fabric into which are woven memories of the past and anticipations of possible futures. Memories of painful experiences of shame can leave dark and indelible marks in such a personal narrative.

A related but contrasting mode of psychological temporality is what I am calling "achronicity." This is a kind of negative mode of temporality, a zero in time, a beginning point in myth and psychological development. This is experienced as timelessness and outside of time frames. Before the number one, which might represent chronicity, there is the number zero, achronicity. Achronicity refers to the absence in consciousness of the sense of objective time ("real time").[2] All takes place is the present tense, and time, if registered at all in this modality, is gossamer-like, a thin veil draped lightly over consciousness but not leaving a deep impression. Here memory may or may not feature as a factor. While the clock continues ticking on the table, the psyche is unaware of its movement. This is experienced by infants, sleepers, daydreamers, deep readers, meditators and mystics, the aged and demented, creative people at work, in short by all of us. If shame registers here, it tends to be vague and generalized, perhaps not attached to specific objects, events, or persons, but rather something more of a mood than a feeling linked to context, and if linked to a specific memory, then to a memory repressed.

Achronicity and chronicity lie on a spectrum with many gradations between the extremes, and they may flow smoothly or roughly into and out of one another. This is depicted by the horizontal axis in Figure 3.1.

The vertical axis is psychologically more complex. The two modes of temporality featured here are able to create some of the deeper wrinkles in the fabric of temporality and may account for shame felt in a strange and impersonal or transgenerational register. The two temporalities on this axis are made up of a complexity of simultaneous time-lines. To become fully aware of them requires observing and remembering one's dreams and fantasies, i.e., the themes and story-lines in the unconscious.

The upward extension of this axis rising above the horizontal line consists of a mode of psychological temporality that Jung named "synchronicity." He refers to this as *acausal correspondences*, which consist in a parallel arrangement of facts in time" (Adler 1975, p. 46). Synchronicity consists in a surprising and unexpected but meaningful convergence of chronological sequences between either: a) the inner world of psyche and the outer world of material objects, or b) two causally unconnected parallel sequences in the material world (for detailed discussions see Atmanspacher 2013; Cambray 2009; Connolly 2015; Jung 1952/1969; Main 2004; Von Franz 1974; Yiassemides 2014). Synchronicity creates a fold in the fabric of temporality that brings together two separate time-lines. Shame may or may not feature prominently in this mode of temporality. Because there is no causal connection between the sequences, no blame can be derived specifically from this twist in time. It is attributed purely to chance: perhaps not to random chance, as Pauli surmised (Pauli 1954/2002, p. 127), but to chance nevertheless.

On the extension downward on the vertical axis is the psychological temporality that I am calling "dyschronicity." This is the contrary of synchronicity, a kind of shadow temporality: two parallel sequences in time are experienced and lived simultaneously but not as convergent. Shame is often embedded here, but often is not of a personal character in that it may be transgenerational.

The problem of shame in the achronicity-chronicity pair of temporality modalities

A. Achronicity

The universe begins from a state of objective achronicity. Time does not exist before the Big Bang, when the material universe exploded into being (Stein 2016, p. 3). Prior to this, there is only a kind of God-alone-space, which in the Mazdean book of Genesis, for instance, is called "the place and abode of Ōhrmazd. Some call it the infinite Light … The Time of the garment [of Ōhrmazd] is infinite" (Corbin 1951/1957, p. 121). Creation myths tell of the moment when the world came into being as taking place *in illo tempore*, "in that time" (Eliade 1958/1968, p. 395). Achronicity is pre-temporal, infinite, and boundless. It is a no-time temporality.

In fact, achronicity is myth's modality of temporality generally. Myth is not contained within chronological time, but rather it contains a time-like feature within it as a kind of internal coherence. Essentially, myth is achronistic in that it does not require historical consciousness or context for meaning. Rather, myth stands alone as "iconic constancy," as Blumenberg observes:

> Iconic constancy is the most characteristic element in the description of myths. The constancy of its core contents allows myth to appear, embedded as an "erratic" element, even in traditional contexts of a different kind ... Its high level of durability ensures its diffusion in time and space, its independence of circumstances of place and epoch. The Greek *mython mytheisthai* [to tell a "myth"] means to tell a story that is not dated and not datable, so that it cannot be localized in any chronicle, but a story that compensates for this lack by being "significant" in itself.
>
> (Blumenthal 1990, p. 149)

While myths exist essentially in achronistic temporality, they do enter into chronicity through being told, heard, and remembered, and thus they take their place within personal and cultural historical narratives and as such can engender cultural or collective shame as in the case of "original sin." On the other hand, rituals are able to transform chronological time into mythical achronicity *in illo tempore* because the ritual, a dance, say, "is a repetition, and consequently a reactualization, of *illud tempus*, 'those days'" (Eliade 1959, pp. 28–9).

"In the beginning ..." (Genesis 1:1), the opening phrase of the Bible, leaves no room for a description of reality "before" the beginning. The Bible begins with the creation of time. Real time did not exist before there were objects in space. Time is a function of the regular rhythms of movements of objects in relation to one another in space. At the moment of creation, the continuous flow of real time can begin because objects now exist. Jung put it as follows: "If there is no body moving in space, there can be no time either ..." (Adler 1975, p. 45). Only the Divine exists outside of time and space, *in illo tempore*, in mythical or imaginal time and space. Divinity (singular and plural) resides within achronistic temporality. This is an eternal present. This also applies to the realm of pure psyche, as Jung writes in a letter: "As in the psychic world there are no bodies moving in space, there is also no time. The archetypal world is 'eternal,' i.e., outside time ..." (Adler 1975, p. 46).

In the biblical account of the beginning, the human sense of time as Adam and Eve experience it remains mythical, or achronistic, even after the six days of creation have been duly counted out and they have taken their place in the Garden of Eden. This indicates the essential difference between human psychic temporality and objective, or real, time. Adam and Eve do not exist within what we would recognize as psychological chronicity, that is, with a sense of time passing continuously from present to future and with a history accumulating in its wake, because they live in an eternal round of day and night without significant change and development. Moreover, they walk and talk easily and regularly directly with God, so there is no division between the human psychic world and the divine archetypal world. Chronistic temporality has not yet begun. While in the Garden of Eden, Adam and Eve live in psychological achronicity, and while this prevails they are without shame. History (i.e., chronicity), which is made of the passage of real time with the conscious linear accumulation of remembered incidents, developments, and changes, begins only after the "fall" and the expulsion from Eden.

In the development of an individual's conscious sense of time, this type of temporality prevails in fetal consciousness and well into the period of infancy. In the modality of psychological achronicity, experiences are registered individually, but because memory is not yet in play they remain unconnected to each other or to contexts in which they took place. In neuroscience this is called "semantic consciousness" (Hinton 2015, p. 363). These are moments registered but not tied together in a continuous narrative by memory.

Humans, if they live long enough and fall into certain pathological neurological conditions like dementia, may end up where they began, in the temporality modality of chronic "achronicity." I vividly recall a scene in an assisted care ward for the demented where two aged men were seated on a bench staring placidly straight ahead into the space in front of them. Across the hallway and in easy eyesight, a clock was ticking and showing the time. Slowly the hands moved on the time-face from number to number. It was early afternoon on a Sunday. The men did not stir from their places. They seemed to be profoundly unaware of time past, present, or future. A sign next to the clock showed that lunch was served daily at 11:30 am. It was now 2:30 pm, so presumably the two men had eaten and were now taking a rest on the bench. Their eyes were wide open, but they did not move even to blink. In whatever state of consciousness they may have been at this moment, it seemed to have no relation to chronological time. They were living in the psychological temporality of perpetual achronicity with no clocks or calendars in mind. Memory no longer functioned to string experiences together. They lived in an eternal present. Their mode of temporality in consciousness was akin to myth and infancy, *in illo tempore*.

Throughout normal healthy life, however, we are also constantly moving between the achronistic mode and a registered sense of chronological time. But we are not stuck in achronicity by neurological deficiency. We can slide along the scale from one position on the horizontal axis to another. When we sleep, when we daydream or fall into reverie, when we meditate or do active imagination, when we gaze blankly into empty space or smell a rose, we are momentarily in achronistic temporality to one degree or another. In fact, most of our days are heavily dotted with achronistic periods, and a careful inventory of consciousness makes it evident that much of our lives are passed in this modality. When time seems to escape us, or the hours on the clock get dramatically compressed and we lose track of hour, day, or year, we are in this mode or perhaps halfway in and halfway out of it. Generally, while awake we slide between achronicity and chronicity easily enough and can move along this axis by acts of will.

The experiences registered within the achronicity modality may include shame stains, but not usually so. An exception is with people strongly embedded in a system of strict rules, often religious laws and mandates that strictly forbid entertaining certain thoughts or feelings. If these surface in achronistic moments (fantasies, dreams, random associations) before they can be repressed and relegated to the basement of unconsciousness, shame will result. For these people, psychotherapy is not an option because they cannot tolerate their shadow affects and thoughts and therefore cannot integrate them. Fear of shame and guilt block the way. The net result is chronic neurotic conflict.

B. Chronicity

In the biblical myth, psychological chronicity begins when Adam and Eve are exiled from the Garden of Eden and the easy flow of conversation between creature and Creator is broken off. The experience of time changes from a round of eternal repetitions of easy-going need-satisfaction cycles to a linear sequence of moments in historical time that demand heavy effort and directed consciousness to proceed from need to fulfillment, with long gaps of frustration often in between. A continuous memory of past events and experiences now takes hold and shapes a narrative as the world begins to change and evolve in human consciousness. In neuroscience this is called the onset of "episodic memory," and it begins for most people around the age of four (Hinton 2015, p. 364). A sense of the future as well, including the awareness of death, takes its place in consciousness. Beginnings and endings take place in chronological time. To live with this sense of temporality is to live in the modality of chronicity.

Adam and Eve, having eaten the fruit of the tree of knowledge of good and evil, leave Eden in shame, and soon enough conflict and power struggles enter the picture. Normal human life begins. Envy gathers like a cloud between their sons, Cain and Abel, and shadow enactments ensue. Crime and punishment become features of human history. The mark of shame becomes indelibly inscribed on the forehead of Cain, the criminal brother, and assumes centrality in his identity. Causal links between past and present and the consequences and responsibilities they entail become the law of life in the temporality modality of chronicity.

I clearly recall that I was four or five years old when my father taught me to tell time. It was an Easter Sunday morning, and before going to church my pastor father gave me a lesson in time. He took a clock about the size of his hand and showed me how the pointers moved could be moved on the face. The small pointer showed the hour, he said, and the large pointer showed the minute. The numbers pointed to indicated the time. I knew enough about time to understand these words. So far, so good. He turned the dial on the back of the clock and made the hands move. Then he set the clock at a certain time and asked me to tell him what time it showed. We did this several times, and soon I got the hang of it. Proudly I announced to my Sunday School friends that I could tell time now! It was a breakthrough in learning for me, and it is a moment in time I have never forgotten. It is a permanent and constant part of my life's narrative. Ever since I have felt that time is my friend, and I rarely lose track of time and am almost never late for meetings and appointments. If I slip up, I feel ashamed. I have a good sense of chronological time and live comfortably within this type of temporality. I am also interested in history that reaches back in time to the origins of human culture and even to the beginnings of the universe, and I place myself within a precise historical and cultural context. Perhaps by coincidence, my earliest memory of experiencing shame dates from about this same age.

At the point in psychological development when chronicity takes permanent hold in consciousness, a separation takes place in the psyche. The emerging ego parts company with the unconscious, and the ego becomes more and more a singular psychic unit unto itself as distinct from other parts of the inner world. The psyche differentiates, in short, and repression begins to occur. Ego defenses form and identity begin to take shape. This birth into chronicity is a kind of second birth of human consciousness, and with this comes the stable awareness of opposites such as good and evil, innocence and shame, success and failure, and life and death. The ego's time sense now becomes one of chronicity, and the psyche's timeless achronicity becomes hidden in the unconscious and left to the world of dreams and fantasy. In childhood, achronicity is restored during play, and creativity throughout life continues to depend on making contact with the ability to play and therefore on temporary re-entry into the mode of achronicity.

In some cultures, notably in those of the East such as Japan, the separation of ego from unconscious is much less drastic and "softer." Myth and history are not as sharply distinguishable, and a normal reality sense may include fantasy importantly in a way that is not the case in the West. Chronicity and achronicity are closer to one another, indeed somewhat intertwined. Here I am following the lines of thought laid down by Hayao Kawai (1988) and Claude Levi-Strauss (2013).

It is worth noting that Japan is known as a "shame-culture" in contrast to the "guilt-cultures" of the West. The anthropologist Ruth Benedict (1946) made this observation initially in her classic work, *The Chrysanthemum and the Sword*. This feature of Japanese culture seems to follow from the closer proximity between achronistic and chronistic modalities of temporality in the population. Some people think that this indicates a lower or lesser level of ego development in this culture because shame is more associated with early ego development while guilt follows more advanced ego development. But in fact shame cannot be separated from guilt as though the latter were a product of greater ego development. As we see in the biblical account of the fall, guilt actually precedes shame, and certainly they come wrapped together in a package. In fact, it is often the case that guilt, as inner self-judgment and condemnation for something done, produces a profound sense of shame.

It has often been argued, too, that guilt is more isolated to a single act in a specific context, whereas shame generalizes to the whole self, but in fact guilt often bleeds beyond the discrete confines of a guilty action and affects the whole psyche-body, including the unconscious. One sees this phenomenon in detail in Dostoyevsky's novel *Crime and Punishment*. Raskolnikov judges himself guilty and thereafter begins to experience excruciating shame in every facet of his being. Paul Ricoeur notes this same development in Kafka's work: "To be accursed without being cursed by anybody is the highest degree of accursedness ..." (Edelman 1998, p. 19). Shame is this "highest degree of accursedness," and it often comes about as the consequence of guilt.

One could say perhaps that in shame-cultures the bleeding from guilt into shame happens more quickly, predictably, and profusely than it does in guilt-cultures. This may be because the ego, which takes responsibility for actions and therefore bears guilt, is not as completely isolated from the rest of the self. The boundary between ego and unconscious is more permeable, and so the experience of shame is more immediate and total. However, this by no means excludes the experience of guilt. Shame and guilt are simply more tightly woven together.

Both shame and guilt enter the psychic picture forcefully with the establishment of the modality of chronicity. In cultures where the chronicity modality is extremely recessive, shame may also be relatively light or even absent. This would be the subject for further research by psychological or cultural anthropology.

As "semantic consciousness" turns into "episodic memory" in a person, a continuous memory takes form and a narrative takes shape made up of associated and linked memories. Of course, this woven together narrative undergoes constant revision in life, and in a sense it must be recreated every day upon awakening from sleep. It is also subject to a process of radical redesign from time to time as a person's life passes through the phases of individuation from childhood to adolescence, adulthood, midlife, old age, and the approach to death. It is not as solid and intact as it might seem at first glance. In fact, upon close inspection it is full of holes and gaps that get filled in from time to time with what Jung called *zurückphantasieren* ("retro-fantasizing") (Laplanche and Pontalis 1973, p. 112) where current feelings and fantasies are transposed and taken for ("remembered" as) past events.[3] In analysis, constant work is done on unweaving and reweaving the narrative based on new insights and emergent memories. A danger here is that this may become nothing more than a sophisticated form of "retro-fantasizing," as has been seen when therapists willfully supported or even inserted vague fantasies in the present into patients' narratives as "memories" of childhood trauma. Early and formative experiences of shame and guilt, of course, naturally take their place in this emerging and constantly transforming narrative of chronicity and assume an important feature there.

The sense of psychological temporality as chronicity is an orientation assumed by consciousness with reference to the material world surrounding us and to our place in it. This is a key function of the "reality principle," as housed with the ego. This modality is a representation in consciousness of temporality as real time ruling over inner or subjective temporalities, which include achronicity, synchronicity, and dyschronicity. When we live with a keen awareness of the clock and calendar and think of ourselves in relation to history, personal and collective, and place ourselves essentially within these contexts, we live in a world where chronicity is king. The ego, oriented by chronicity, is the sun around which all other temporalities revolve. The development in this direction begins early in life and lasts throughout, as long as one remains sound of mind. Mental status tests look to this as a key feature of sanity. Psychosis is a break in the dominance of chronicity within consciousness, when other forms of temporality take over and the ego loses its central place. Then subjective factors like feelings, thoughts, and fantasies assume dominance, and with them come other temporality modalities such as achronicity (dementia), synchronicity (paranoia), and dyschronicity (dissociation) to replace the ego's grasp on chronicity and real time.

The sense of the world and life as strictly determined by chronicity has great advantages for humankind, and it includes a sense of human life as developmental and finite. One is aware of the inevitability of death, and one monitors one's age more carefully as the probabilities for the end of one's personal history increase. This psychological temporality mode introduces and holds shame and guilt into consciousness, and along with this come necessarily the appearance of ethics and the elaboration of moral rules. Ethics depends on an awareness of object relations and causality in time and space.

Human culture depends on psychological chronicity as a powerful and indeed dominant fact of consciousness. In a sense, an acute awareness of shame is a price we pay for culture.

The Synchronicity-Dyschronicity Pair of Temporality Modalities

C. Synchronicity

The type of temporality modality that Adam and Eve live within while in the Garden of Eden is achronistic (mythical), but it is also synchronistic: In Eden, there is complete and smooth harmony between supply and demand, between inner need and outer fulfillment, between psyche and world. This is the archetypal template for temporality in the modality of synchronicity, when inner (psyche) and outer (objective world) are in a harmonious and syntonic relationship. In this state of consciousness, there is no sense of shame. Synchronicity in itself is shame-free, but if it is taken up into the chronicity of the ego's normal experience of life and considered in a different light, perhaps ethical, it may take on an aspect of shame.

Synchronicity refers to an acausal or chance falling together in time of the inner (image, thought, feeling) and the outer (material objects, creatures), and objective meaning is revealed in the event (Jung 1952/1969). It is a coincidental and meaningful confluence of psyche and matter, inner and outer, subjective and objective temporalities. The timing of the psyche, conscious or unconscious, and the timing of events in the objective world by chance simply happen by chance to coincide meaningfully. Two lines of temporality in this instance become intertwined as one within consciousness.

Erich Neumann writes of infancy in terms that imply this same type of syntony between inner and outer worlds. The fetus while contained in the mother's womb passes this stage of life in a state of achronicity. After birth this gradually passes over into what later in her arms and at her breast becomes a prefiguration of the synchronistic state:

> This childhood experience … is the ontogenetic embodiment of the primal unitary reality in which the partial worlds of outside and inside, objective world and psych do not exist … In this phase there is a primary unity of mother and child.
>
> (Neumann 1973/2002, p. 11)

Here nature facilitates the closely coordinated timing of need and satisfaction, as mother's acts of feeding and infant's need to be fed are more or less well timed to coincide. The inner is met by the outer in a timely fashion when infant cries and mother responds. This is a personal prototype of temporality as synchronicity: psyche and world are in a state of syntony. For development, this is a transitional state moving from achronicity to chronicity, and it is, like the Original Parents, without shame.

An early and preverbal experience of shame may occur in this phase of infant development, however, if the expressed need is not met or the mirroring of mother fails to meet the gaze of the infant. Edelman, referring to the work of Kaufman, writes: "Facial gazing is … the earliest form of communion. If the fundamental expectations are not met during this activity, shame is constellated" (Edelman 1998, p. 29). Since this occurs within the psychological temporality of achronicity, however, it does not become carried forward in time and woven into the narrative of memory. It will simply remain an experience of shame unassociated to time or place, and since the context is missing it will be akin to what Bion called beta elements, which do not get psychically metabolized. If repeated often enough, these early experiences of shame may become the foundation for generalized sense of shame, or basic fault (Balint 1968/1979), in the sense of self, a primal wound that does not heal and creates a free-floating and pervasive undertone of shame in a person's moods later in life. They may become what Jung calls a complex, a complex of shame. This would be attributable to the breakdown of synchronistic meetings of inner and outer, infant and mother, need and satisfaction, in the early developmental process.

The experience of syntony that comes out of the synchronistic match-ups between infant and mother is objectively meaningful in that it supports the healthy survival of the species. The beneficiaries of good enough mothering are more fit than those who do not have this experience. This will lay the ground for later optimism and faith, qualities of mind that are good for thriving in later life. This foundational experience of syntony in infancy is a personal template for later experiences of synchronicity, which reflects the archetypal Edenic one. The later experiences of synchronicity, which take place and are recorded into memory after the ego has been formed and inner and outer worlds have been separated, show similar coincidences between need and satisfaction, inner and outer worlds, in a meaningful way.

The overlapping of chronicities, inner with outer, that takes place in synchronicity also brings the perception of transcendent meaning to a specific moment in time. The experience of temporality as synchronistic is therefore sometimes referred to as *kairos* (a kind of elevated or spiritually significant season or period of time) as opposed to *chronos* (ordinary sequential time). Hinton references Andre Green as speaking of "moments of breakthrough of temporality ... or 'exploded time ...'" in which "the strictures of time are 'exploded', and a more 'open ensemble' of psychic life emerges" (Hinton 2015, p. 358). This is a lovely poetic description of synchronicity temporality. Connolly describes several such synchronistic experiences in the clinical setting in similar terms (Connolly 2015, pp. 167ff.). On a more mythological note, Von Franz writes about this phenomenon that "*kairos* signifies the 'right order' in time. The association of *kairos* with goddesses weaving time alludes ... to the idea of a 'field' in which 'meaningful connections' are interwoven like threads in a fabric" (Von Franz 1974, p. 256).

D. Dyschronicity

Because conscious and unconscious are separated in the human psyche after a point in psychological development, there is a strong possibility that the timing between them becomes disconnected. This is the usual neurotic condition that we confront in analysis. Instead of experiencing a state of simple chronicity in consciousness or one of achronicity or synchronicity, a state of dyschronicity prevails either subtly or blatantly. Two different time programs, instead of falling "together, with" as in synchronicity, form a disconnected parallel sequence and create a mismatch of temporalities in the psyche. They remain apart and are often quite unconnected in consciousness. A contradiction between one aspect of psyche's time and another occurs, with the result that there is a type of dystonia, a more or less severe lack of coordination, in the temporality system as a whole. There creates a deep wrinkle in the fabric of temporality, which may be registered in consciousness or not. When it becomes conscious, a possibility exists for working with this conflict or dissociation in analysis.

For years I have been fascinated by a passage in Jung's late autobiographical work, *Memories, Dreams, Reflections,* where he recounts the experience of living in two different centuries, the 17th and the 20th, at the same time.

> It was wartime. I was on the Italian front and driving back from the front line with a little man, a peasant, in his horse-drawn wagon … We had to cross a bridge and then go through a tunnel … Arriving at the end of the tunnel, we saw before us a sunny landscape, and I recognized the region around Verona … The road led through lovely springtime countryside … Then, diagonally across the road, I caught sight of a large building, a manor house of grand proportions, rather like the palace of a North Italian duke … The little coachman and myself drove in through a gate, and from here we could see, through a second gate at the far end, the sunlit landscape again … Just as we reached the middle of the courtyard, in front of the main entrance, something unexpected happened: with a dull clang, both gates flew shut. The peasant leaped down from his seat and exclaimed, "Now we are caught in the seventeenth century." Resignedly I thought, "Well, that's that! But what is there to do about it? Now we shall be caught for years." Then the consoling thought came to me: "Someday, years from now, I shall get out again." … Not until much later did I realize that it [i.e., the dream] referred to alchemy, for that science reached its height in the seventeenth century.
>
> (Jung/Jaffe 1961/1989, pp. 202–3)

This dream reflects a strange doubling in Jung's sense of temporality, even an acute disturbance, and it echoes his childhood feeling of living with two personalities, Number One located in the present time, and Number Two in the 18th century (Jung/Jaffe 1961/1989, pp. 23–83).[4] In his waking life at the time of this dream (1926), he was a highly successful middle-aged professional and family man of the 20th century, but in his dream retreats in time from WWI and is eventually locked into the 17th century. There signifies a large gap between the temporality lived in everyday conscious life by the steady beat of a reliable Swiss watch and the temporality of his unconscious as registered in this impressive dream, a discrepant doubling of Jung's sense of temporal identity into two seemingly disconnected time frames. Inner and outer temporalities are hugely discrepant. It is a dystonic state at first and totally uncoordinated. Later it will become extremely meaningful. This particular dream, which may well have had a long prehistory in his unconscious as indicated in his memories of a childhood with two personalities separated in time by centuries as well, made a deep impression on the mature Jung and drove him to a sense of mission that would take years to complete. He worked mightily to reconcile these two overlaid temporalities in his identity, even into his advanced years.[5] It was a dyschronicity that made a difference.

One can find many examples of dyschronicity in literature and in life. Nostalgia is a form of dyschronicity if taken to the extreme of living simultaneously in two time periods. William Faulkner was a master storyteller of this psychological condition. One found this condition floridly lived out in the American "old south" where many people continued to live well into the 20th century in the long bygone days of wine and roses of the pre-civil war period. Cervantes' novel *Don Quixote* offers a humorous and touching example of a character living within two temporalities simultaneously, his current and mundane time period and the romantic days of knights and ladies of centuries before. Like Jung, he lives in two disparate temporalities. Unlike Jung, he does not manage to bring them together in a meaningful way, although he does in the end break out of his delusion. An example from film is Woody Allen's marvelous comedy *Midnight in Paris*. By day the protagonist lives in the 21st century, and by night he finds himself in the Paris of the 1920s where his adventures are far more colorful and concordant than his daytime life. The film brilliantly resolves the conflict that gathers as a result of this dyschronicity. An example of dyschronicity from the manuals of psychopathology is the paraphilia known as *autoneplophilia*, or adult baby syndrome. Here a person in the body of an adult simultaneously chooses to remain in an infant's psyche. Adult and baby co-inhabit the ego's sense of temporality.[6] Another form of this is the refusal to accept the body's aging. Cosmetic surgeons thrive on this form of psychological dyschronicity. People live two lives: one in an aging body, and another in the cosmetized body of a youthful psyche. This discrepancy can lead to spasmodic episodes of shame because fantasy images of self and the reality of one's body do not match. Thus shame gets woven into the fabric of temporality via dyschronicity.

Two cases of dyschronicity

In analytical practice we may come upon the phenomenon of dys-chronicity as we delve into the unconscious and discover autonomous complexes at work in the psyche. Viktor, a Swiss man in his mid-fifties, told me a dream early in his analysis. He said that he dreamed of being attacked by a group of wild natives, "primitives," in a far-away foreign country. This took place in what seemed like another century. He was traveling by horse-drawn wagon through a high desert area with a few other people when suddenly they noticed on the ridges above them and up ahead the figures of a large number of threatening half-clad men preparing to attack their party. He awoke in a panic, and he now described this to me as a nightmare similar to others of being attacked he had experienced in the past. He had no particular associations to the primitive attackers or to the setting of the dream, other than from the movies, and nothing in his recent past suggested an image like this one. There was no specific residue from the previous days. It was a strange and puzzling dream, obviously symbolic. I thought about the transference even though this did not fit with anything we had experi-enced up to this early point in the analysis, but I took it to be a signal of possible trouble ahead. At this point, it was as though this dream belonged to another person, in another time and place, and with no connection to the dreamer, a European man through and through who had never traveled in such areas of the world. There was a time dis-junction between his waking consciousness and the dream scene, as though it had happened in an earlier century and to another self.

The dream shows a large discontinuity between the dreamer's con-scious life in the present, where normal chronicity rules and where he was appropriately oriented to reality and generally competent in his various activities, and his inner life in the temporality of the uncon-scious operating in psychic time. Two distinct and discrepant tempor-alities are running their programs, the one current in his present life and the other far in the past of previous generations. As further analysis revealed, this was a dissociation that formed as a result of many early childhood traumas. These traumas were largely split off from his ego-consciousness and were hidden behind his upper middle class social identity as a husband, father, and active businessman. In actuality, he was living in a psychic set-up that was severely uncoordinated between his ego's time and his unconscious time and its complexes. As a child, he had never felt safe for a variety of reasons, and so his defenses then and now in adulthood were hypervigilant and ever at the ready to protect himself from abuse and attack. The unconscious scene of being under attack vividly portrayed the difficulties that had brought him into analysis: explosive and sudden defensive rage attacks, violent reactions at little or no provocation, disruptive anxieties of an irrational nature, and frequent breakdowns in relationships with intimate others. The dream image pictures a split-off feeling-toned complex with the usual polarities: a surprised and innocent victim, and abusive attackers. In an uncanny way, this scene would be repeated regularly in Viktor's life.

An activated complex means that past events can suddenly overshadow the present in the emotional life of a person and often generate highly overcharged and inappropriate reactions. In Victor's life this would happen when a waiter accidentally spilled a cup of coffee or the housemaid failed to clean his bathroom properly. In these instances, the complex would discharge an amount of affect that would better be used in an extreme situation like the scene pictured in his dream. Suddenly, chronicity would give way to dyschronicity, and what was simply an accident or an oversight would be interpreted as a life-threatening attack.

In time, his dreams became more explicitly relevant to Viktor's present life and his emotional reactions to situations in the present better attuned to actual temporality in the present. The two temporality systems began to converge, and modulation of emotion could be better achieved. The childhood traumas became memories and could be largely integrated into his autobiographical narrative. Dyschronicity was reduced, a sense of routine chronicity in waking life was strengthened, and synchronicity could emerge in the appearances of meaningful coordination between psyche and world in his everyday life.

An important side effect of this gradual integration was that a sense of shame actually developed and grew stronger as present temporality replaced dyschronicity. The outbursts were no longer dissociated and so had to be acknowledged. As chronicity replaced dyschronicity, shame entered the psychic field and led to the possibility of apology and reparation. Thus we see again that shame is linked to temporality as chronicity. As Hinton has suggested, shame may become a teacher for culture and individuation (Hinton 1999).

Another case of dyschronicity, similar to Viktor's in some respects, but considerably more severe and painful, was that of Gertrude, a highly sensitive German analysand in her 60s. The relevant part of this story is that she had previously decided to explore a form of intense regression therapy that had left her with a broken sense of self from which she could not recover. What she had "remembered" and powerfully experienced in that therapy was the trauma of being a Jew in Nazi Germany and being sent with her young daughter to a death camp. There she had been separated from her and knew that the girl had been violently raped and brutally murdered. Even though she had survived the camp by some quirk of fate, she was left utterly bereft and did not know how to continue her life in the face of such evil and loss. When Gertrude came to see me, she was still mired in a deep depression. She felt that her life had been irrevocably changed by the experience of a "past life." She was living in two time frames. In the present, she was a fairly comfortably well-off professional woman with a healthy family; in the past, she was a devastated camp survivor. The sense of this tragic and horrifying past utterly overshadowed her present. She was depressed, anxious, and without hope for anything of positive value in the future. She was suffering from a memory of a life that was not hers, at least not in the chronicity temporality modality of her life.

The telling fact behind this case of dyschronicity was that in the previous generations her parents and grandparents had been complicit in the Holocaust. Even though their participation in the events of those times was largely indirect, the collective guilt for what had happened infected them, but largely at unconscious levels. Therefore they could not speak about it even if they had wished to do so. Today therapists recognize the effects of "transgenerational transmission of trauma" (Schellinski 2014), and this was such a case. The paradox was that the transmission of collective guilt, inherited by Gertrude as a cultural complex (Singer and Kaplinski 2010), had been reversed so that she now experienced the suffering of the victims rather than the guilt of the perpetrators. Shame and guilt had been transformed into the opposite, into innocent suffering, not in order to escape the shame primarily, in my opinion, but to expiate the cultural guilt through vicarious suffering. This was the meaning of dyschronicity in this case. Gertrude had to bear the suffering inflicted on the victims of earlier generations of perpetrators. Dyschronicity had found a permanent home in Gertrude's consciousness, and no amount of reductive analysis could remove it. It had to be borne as though it were her suffering, added to which was the shadow of survivor guilt since she had escaped execution. Grasping the suffering in this way would make it possible for her to search out meaning in it, for herself and for her generation. Here, too, shame and guilt, as Hinton has suggested (Hinton 1999), could become enlisted in the project of individuation.

A further reflection on temporality and the problem of shame – the role of the transcendent function

Figure 3.2 shows the four modalities of temporality feeding into a central psychic agency, ego-consciousness.

As the center of consciousness, the ego may register the four modalities, and with maturity it is able to contain them and include them in a coherent narrative. Jung's autobiography, *Memories, Dreams, Reflections*, for instance, includes all four modalities in the narrative. For purposes of further analysis, I have assigned a numerical value to each of the temporalities as follows: pure achronicity is given the value of Zero, indicating the emptiness of chronological consciousness in this modality; the chronicity modality is given the value of One, signifying full consciousness of chronological time as a single flowing stream of events from past to present to future; the modality of synchronicity is

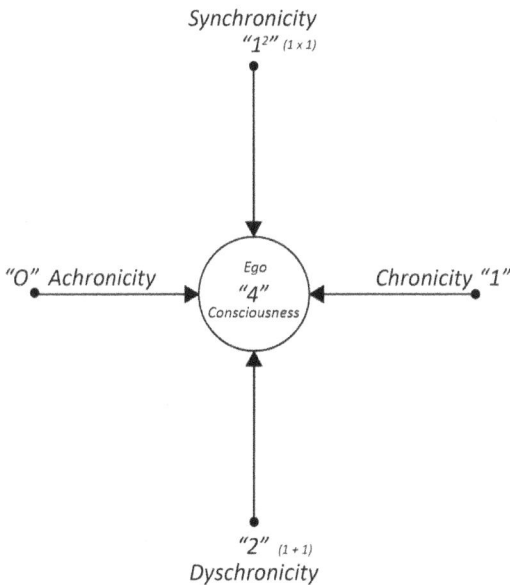

Figure 3.2 Times four

assigned the numerical value of one squared, again One, but with two parallel chronicities twisted into a single moment of chronological time; the dyschronicity modality is given the value of Two, which indicates two temporalities running in parallel but separated in the psyche. At the center, within an ego-consciousness aware of all four modalities these numerical values add up to the number Four. The ego is the container, too, of whatever stains of shame blemish the fabric of a personal narrative, provided they are conscious and not repressed or forgotten. These stains (both conscious and unconscious) may derive from pre-verbal early infancy or other periods of pure achronicity in life (the achronicity arm), from experiences within the chronological memory of the person (the chronicity arm), from transpersonal sources (the synchronicity arm), and from transgenerational transmissions (the dyschronicity arm). All of these stains of shame may be collected by the central agency of consciousness and combined into the total narrative of person's history. This is a person who has faced the shadow, made it conscious, and is able to carry this as memory in consciousness. For such a person, shame will be a teacher of humility. This is an advanced stage of individuation, hence it attains to the number Four.

The problem of complete integration of the modalities themselves remains, however. The ego is able to count them and to reflect on them but not by its own efforts to integrate them. Integration means unification, or what Jung in his late writing on alchemy called "conjunction" from the Latin phrase *mysterium coniunctionis* ("mystical conjunction"), the title of his last major work. For unification or conjunction to take place, a larger and more powerful agency is required, one that can embrace the opposites, i.e., the two pairs of temporality modality, and contain them as facets of a single unit of a superior psychological structure.

Our reflection on this high degree of integration of the four modalities and the contents they bring with them into the fabric of temporality will border on the ontological and the theological. This level of deep integration is symbolized by Pauli at the conclusion of his "Piano Lesson" by the golden "Ring i," which is presented to him in the narrative by his female teacher.

It is a mandala with the mathematical symbol i at the center. This symbol, i, is an imaginary unit that opens up new dimensions within mathematical fields so that "complex numbers" can be created, which combine real and imaginary numbers. The symbol i is a sort of magical unifier of opposites, in alchemical terms a Mercurius figure. The golden "ring i" transforms the center of identity, previously occupied by the ego, and replaces the dominance of chronistic temporality with a synthetic union of all four modalities.

Figure 3.3 "The Ring *i*"

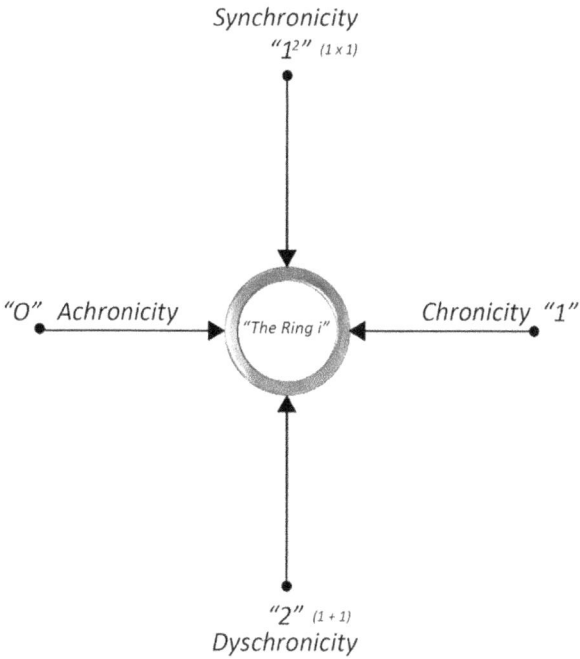

Synchronicity
"1^2" (1×1)

"O" *Achronicity*   "The Ring i"   *Chronicity* "1"

"2" $(1 + 1)$
Dyschronicity

Figure 3.4 Times Four with the Ring *i*

"It makes time into a static image," Pauli exclaims to his teacher (Pauli 1954/2002, p. 134). In the terms used in this essay, it transcends the four modalities of temporality and folds them into a single unit or monad. It is a symbol of the self, the central agency of the psyche as a whole and superordinate to the ego. Figure 3.4 illustrates the constellation of the self and represents the installation of the ego-self axis (Neumann 1952/1989) at the center of consciousness.

This constellation of the ego-self axis introduces the timeless into consciousness alongside the temporality modalities, not to replace them but to accompany them as an overtone. Von Franz concludes her book, *Time, Rhythm and Repose*, with the same perception: "from the timeless God flows the 'flow of grace' which creates an ever-present now – so that God is simultaneously stillness and everlasting flux" (Von Franz 1978, p. 31). The dialectical play between the ego and the self accounts for this simultaneity. Von Franz shows the levels of temporality and their arrangement in Figure 3.5, which also indicates the displacement of the ego from the center to the periphery while the self assumes the position of center, or "sun," around which the ego revolves.

"Ego-time" in this diagram is chronicity in the personal sphere, while "aeonic time" is chronicity extended to larger frameworks of chronological time such as the Platonic year consisting of 2,000 years, which are called Aeons. "*Illud Tempus*" is mythic time and

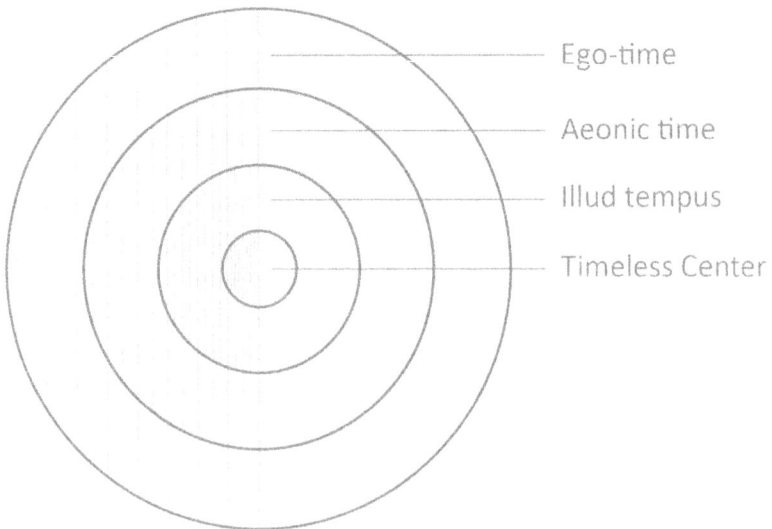

Figure 3.5 Levels of temporality

therefore achronistic, the framework in which the archetypes reside and execute their wills by creating synchronicities and dyschronicities in real time. "The timeless centre" is the self and equivalent to Pauli's Ring *i,* where time becomes "a static image." As such, it is a transcendent agency beyond the temporalities but with a creative impact on time through initiating synchronistic phenomena ("acts of creation in time" – Jung) via the various lesser archetypal agencies. The symbol, "Ring *i,*" includes recognition of reciprocity between ego and self such that they interact with one another dynamically and drive an evolutionary process forward in human consciousness.

What is the effect of the constellation of the ego-self axis on the shame stains in the temporality handkerchief? So long as sheer temporality in its various modalities dominates consciousness exclusively, shame remains, although in a pure achronicity modality it may tend to fade into the vacuum left by the absence of memory. But assuming that the four modalities remain intact and are subsumed by the self constellation, by the Ring *i*, what happens to shame?

Returning to the biblical narrative, running from the myth of Adam and Eve in the Book of Genesis onward through the entire Bible, the problem of shame and guilt ("sin") remains indelibly a feature of the human condition. Once chronistic temporality takes hold, shame becomes resident in consciousness and remains. This is human reality. The handkerchief is stained, and as time passes it gets more and more so and crumpled by the fluctuating temporality modalities. In the biblical view, the stain can be somewhat reduced by strict obedience to the Mosaic Law and by observance of its vast array of ethical implications, but it cannot be removed, and constantly it threatens to expand and deepen. In fact, the application of the Law increases the sense of sin because it raises consciousness of personal and individual as well as collective responsibility. The fall from grace into shame and the consequent expulsion from the Garden of Eden created a radical and permanent blemish in humanity, which had originally been created in the image of God (*imago Dei*), and this called for a radical solution.

Such a solution is offered in the New Testament. When Christ, as the New Adam, replaces the Old Adam he restores the *imago Dei* in a singular human being to its original state of perfection. In Christ, there is no element of sin, no shame, despite his having entered into temporality as an ordinary flesh-and-blood human being. Mythic purity is restored because Christ is also Divine. The Christian solution to the problem of shame then takes form in the possibility of making an identification with the Christ figure. The stain is washed clean in the

Christ symbol, and this can be transmitted to the believer through identification with Him. With relief, St. Paul cries out: "Wretch that I am, who will rescue me from this doomed body? Thanks be to God – [it is done] through Jesus Christ our Lord!" (Romans 7:24–5; Fitzmyer 1993, p. 472). Following shortly upon the Ascension of Christ, the descent of the Holy Spirit on the Day of Pentecost and the reception of the spirit into human consciousness created a new spiritual center in the psyche of the believers (Acts 2:4). In the mystical language of St. Paul: "it is no longer I who live, but Christ who lives in me" (Galatians 2:20). The Christians, as they now were called, no longer lived out of a chronicity-dominated ego but out of a transcendent spiritual identity associated with Christ. The blemished, folded, and crumpled handkerchief of temporality was washed clean and transformed into a spiritualized fabric. Temporality lost its power, in the view of the early Christians. Christ has conquered the power of temporality, as they would affirm.

In this religious narrative of release from all modalities of temporality and the shame that becomes resident in consciousness with them, the psyche is seen as having recovered a transcendent center in consciousness, whence it originated as *imago Dei*, rather than maintaining its primary residence exclusively in the alienated ego that developed in history. Psychologically, this possibly represents an advanced stage of individuation and not a regression, provided that the ego-self axis is constellated in the center of consciousness and the dialectic between ego and self is maintained. If the ego does not vanish into the void of unconsciousness but rather becomes subordinated to a larger agency through the "transcendent function" (Jung 1916/1969), then a reciprocal relationship between ego and self replaces the ego alone as the center of consciousness. This creates a kind of dual identity with a binary structure. Here time and the timeless walk together, the secular person and the sacred. The problem of shame within the fabric of temporality is partially resolved, therefore by being taken up as a part of the larger self, which as a union of opposites is able to integrate, i.e., *unify*, the light and the dark, the innocent and the shameful, and the temporal and the eternal into a unique singularity. This translates into a state of self-acceptance. As Paul Tillich announced in his famous sermon, "You Are Accepted": "Accept that you are accepted … You are accepted. *You are accepted*, accepted by that which is greater than you, and the name of which you do not know" (Tillich 1948, p. 162). Many mystical traditions, such as Cabbala, Hasidism (Magid 2015), Sufism, Yoga, Zen Buddhism (Izutsu 1977) and others, have made identical moves toward transcending temporality even if only momentarily. This is a goal of individuation as conceived by Jung and those following him in depth psychology. All arrive at the position symbolized by Pauli's "Ring *i*," a place beyond sheer temporality and shame and characterized by compassion, grace, and a sense of wholeness realized.

From a realistic and psychological point of view, it is wise, however, to think of this goal of individuation as something sought for and attained momentarily from time to time in experiences of ego-transcendence. The return to temporality, and especially to the chronicity modality, is inevitable and often abrupt. Humans, as long as they live and breathe in a physical body, continue to live in temporality and therefore with the problem of shame. Within temporality, shame can become a guide and counselor, as Hinton describes, functioning to keep the human ego aware of its finite condition and its limitations. Shame is endemic and built into human experience because we live in the temporalities. In that sense, shame is "ontological," that is to say, it is archetypal, and therefore built into the structure of human experience. Because the ego-self axis is constructed dialectically, there is a continual interaction between time and eternity. To think of a permanent escape from temporality and shame while in this life is a dangerous illusion and leads to utopian fantasies that inevitably collapse and produce only further experiences of ever-deeper shame.

Notes

1 I have created this neologism for the purposes of this chapter. To my knowledge, no one has discussed this phenomenon before, although it well known among Jungian psychoanalysts. I chose the prefix dys- (from Gr. meaning bad, hard, unlucky) because it indicates a difficult, often abnormal, and sometimes painful state.

2 I use the phrase "real time" to indicate time as measured by clocks, i.e., objective time, which exists beyond human recognition of it. It is non-psychological temporality.

3 Hinton offers a useful discussion of *Nachträglichkeit*, the revision of memory in light of reflections back on earlier experiences such as early childhood traumas. See Hinton (2015, p. 361ff).

4 This perception of having two very different temporal personalities organizes the entire chapter on childhood titled "School Years."

5 Jung's last great work, *Mysterium Coniunctionis* (Collected Works 14), is the culmination of this project.

6 The only instance of a Jungian discussion of this paraphilia, to my knowledge, is a paper by the late Prof. Leland Roloff (1992) in his Chicago IAAP Congress lecture.

Bibliography

Adler, G. (ed.) (1975). *C.G. Jung Letters* (Vol. 2). Princeton, NJ: Princeton University Press.

Atmanspacher, H. (2013). A structural-phenomenological typology of the mind-matter correlations. *Journal of Analytical Psychology*, 58/2, 219–245.

Balint, M. (1968/1979). *The Basic Fault*. New York: Brunner/Mazel.

Benedict, R. (1946). *The Chrysanthemum and the Sword: Patterns of Japanese Culture*. Boston: Houghton Mifflin.

Blumenberg, H. (1990). *Work on Myth*. Cambridge, MA and London: MIT Press.

Corbin, H. (1951/1957). Cyclical time in Mazdaism and Ismailism. In J. Campbell (ed.), *Man and Time*. Princeton, NJ: Princeton University Press, pp. 115–172.

Cambray, J. (2009). *Synchronicity: Nature and Psyche in an Interconnected Universe*. College Station, TX: Texas A & M University Press.

Connolly, A. (2015). Bridging the reductive and the synthetic: some reflections on the clinical implications of synchronicity. *Journal of Analytical Psychology*, 60/2, 159–178.

Edelman, S.P. (1998). *Turning the Gorgon: A Meditation on Shame*. Woodstock, CT: Spring Publications.

Eliade, M. (1958/1968). *Patterns in Comparative Religion*. Cleveland, OH: The World Publishing Company.

Eliade, M. (1959). *Cosmos and History: The Myth of the Eternal Return*. New York: Harper Torchbooks.

Fitzmyer, J. (1993). *Romans. The Anchor Yale Bible*. New Haven and London: Yale University Press.

Hinton, L. (1999). Shame as a teacher. In M.A. Mattoon (ed.), *Florence 1998 – Destruction and Creation*. Einsiedeln: Daimon Verlag, pp. 172–185.

Hinton, L. (2015). Temporality and the torments of time. *Journal of Analytical Psychology*, 60/3, 353–370.

Izutsu, T. (1977). *Toward a Philosophy of Zen Buddhism*. Boulder, CO: Prajna Press.

Jung, C.G. (1916/1969). The transcendent function. In *The Collected Works of C.G. Jung* (Vol. 8). Princeton, NJ: Princeton University Press.

Jung, C.G. (1944/1968). Psychology and alchemy. In *The Collected Works of C.G. Jung* (Vol. 12). Princeton, NJ: Princeton University Press.

Jung, C.G. (1952/1969). Synchronicity: An acausal connecting principle. In *The Collected Works of C.G, Jung* (Vol. 8). Princeton, NJ: Princeton University Press.

Jung, C.G., with Jaffé, A. (1961/1989). *Memories, Dreams, Reflections*. New York: Random House.

Kawai, H. (1988). *The Japanese Psyche*. Dallas, TX: Spring Publications.

Kaufman, G. (1989). *The Psychology of Shame*. New York: Springer Publishing Company.

Laplanche, J. and Pontalis, J.-B. (1973). *The Language of Psycho-Analysis*. New York: Norton.

Levi-Strauss, C. (2013). *The Other Face of the Moon*. Cambridge, MA and London: The Belknap Press of Harvard University Press.

Magid, S. (2015). *Hasidism Incarnate: Hasidism, Christianity, and the Construction of Modern Judaism*. Stanford, CA: Stanford University Press.

Main, R. (2004). *The Rupture of Time: Synchronicity and Jung's Critique of Modern Western Culture*. Hove & New York: Brunner-Routledge.

Neumann, E. (1952/1989). The psyche and the transformation of the reality planes. In *The Place of Creation*. Princeton, NJ: Princeton University Press, pp. 3–62.

Neumann, E. (1973/2002). *The Child*. London: Karnac Books.

Pauli, W. (1954/2002). The piano lesson. *Harvest*, 49/2, 122–134.

Roloff, L. (1992). Living, ignoring, and regressing. In *Chicago 92*. Einsiedeln: Daimon Verlag, pp. 195–211.

Schellinski, K. (2014). Horror inherited: Transgenerational transmission of collective trauma in dreams. In G. Gudaité and M. Stein (eds.), *Confronting Cultural Trauma*. New Orleans, LA: Spring Journal Books, pp. 11–30.

Singer, T. and Kaplinski, C. (2010). Cultural complexes in analysis. In M. Stein (ed.), *Jungian Psychoanalysis*. Chicago, IL: Open Court, pp. 22–37.

Stein, M. (2006). *The Principle of Individuation*. Wilmette, IL: Chiron Publications.

Stein, M. (2014). *Minding the Self: Jungian Meditations on Contemporary Spirituality*. London & New York: Routledge.

Stein, M. (2016). On synchronizing time and eternity. *International Journal of Jungian Studies*, 8/1, 1–14.

Tillich, P. (1948). *The Shaking of the Foundations*. New York: Charles Scribner's Sons.

Von Franz, M.-L. (1974). *Number and Time*. Evanston, IL: Northwestern University Press.

Von Franz, M.-L. (1978). *Time: Rhythm and Repose*. New York: Thames and Hudson.

Von Franz, M.-L. (1992). *Psyche and Matter*. Boston & London: Shambhala.

Yiassmides, A. (2014). *Time and Timelessness: Temporality in the Theory of Carl Jung*. London and New York: Routledge.

Chapter 4

Reflections on Murray Stein's paper "The four modalities of temporality and the problem of shame"

Synchronicity as the bridge between achronicity and chronicity

Elena Caramazza

Preludes to synchronicity

I would like to discuss above all the passage in your paper concerning the temporality that is called "synchronicity," since I was particularly struck by it. If I have understood correctly, the synchronicity that is experienced in infancy and linked to the mother's capacity to respond empathically to a baby's needs has a dual function: on the one hand, it allows a person who has reached maturity to recognize truly synchronic events, in which two temporal sequences linked not by a causal nexus but one of meaning occur in parallel in the outside and inside worlds; on the other, it teaches the infant how to emerge from the total domination of an achronicity temporality modality, to enter chronicity and gradually acquire the capacity to fix individual memories and organize them in a continuous memory. Might we say, therefore, that synchronicity, at least as a precocious experience, constitutes the bridge that enables the transition from achronicity to chronicity and coordinates these two temporality modalities? If so, this would create a continuum between achronicity and chronicity that would permit us to temporarily immerse ourselves in the achronistic modality and, rather than remaining trapped in it, to discover that we are capable of restoring to continuous consciousness its hidden treasures and profound mysteries.

We might also say – as, in fact, you explain so clearly – that when the syntony between mother and infant (and hence between psyche and world) is prevented or brusquely interrupted, the ensuing feeling of shame does not lead to an awareness of blame, of error, or of a sense of responsibility for our actions and their consequences, especially when the latter are damaging to us and others. Then, shame becomes a pervasive sense of unworthiness, inadequacy, nullity almost, which makes us isolate ourselves, break off all relationships, withdraw from life and history, and experience a compelling need to remain "unborn" – I shall include below a brief account of a clinical experience regarding this.

However, I would like to begin by exploring this topic further through a childhood memory of mine that re-emerged while I was reading the part of your paper where you recall your father teaching you to tell time, which actually marked the beginning of chronistic temporality for you. I must also have been about four or five when my imagination was particularly struck by a certain event. I had recently been wondering why my mind would go blank when adults asked me "Do you remember that time ...?" Then I asked myself why we forget, and decided to fix an episode in my memory, after which I would never have forgotten anything. It consisted in the following scene, which lent itself to my purpose because I found it so meaningful: I was in our house in Tuscany, where I used to spend the summer with the family because my father had various work commitments in the region. We had a large garden, part of which was uncultivated, and a cat had chosen to give birth to her kittens in the most overgrown corner! She was not a house-cat and every time anyone went near her she would either run away or react furiously. One day I was sitting with my nanny by the steps that led to the basement floor, where there was a room for storing firewood. Suddenly, the cat appeared and carried her kittens by the scruff, one by one, into the room below, passing right in front of us every time without showing any fear. I was terrified she would hurt her young by biting them on the neck, but my nanny calmed my fears, explaining that this was how mother cats usually transported their kittens. Obviously, I did not understand why the cat had confronted what she saw as a "human danger" and taken her kittens into the house. At that particular moment the sky was blue, there was not a cloud in sight, and the sun was shining brightly, but after a few minutes, perhaps half an hour at the most, the atmosphere darkened and there was a terrible storm with thunder, lightning, and heavy downpours. It was then that I realized that the cat had brought her kittens inside to save them from mortal danger, because the rainstorm posed far more of a threat to them than we humans.

Reliving that memory now, in the light of your considerations, I would say I witnessed an event that combined the modalities of synchronicity and chronicity, which was precisely why it was able to mark the beginning of my memory continuity. In fact, I can now reconstruct the profound meaning that this had for me, because the synchronicity I had experienced in infancy, during the months of syntony with my mother, was brusquely interrupted when she suffered a terrible bereavement that enclosed her in a shell of grief, distancing her from everything and everyone. I think I can reconstruct a posteriori (I was only nine months old when it happened) that I experienced an all-pervasive feeling of shame: there had to be something wrong with me, I must have done something very bad for her to have abandoned me. The episode of the young mother cat enabled me to enter chronistic time precisely because it offered me the possibility to reconstruct the torn fabric of my early experience of synchronicity by presenting me with the image and experience of a mother who protected her young, who heeded their plea for help, and responded by providing the state of security that is the foundation of life.

Indeed, if we analyze the episode it is clear that the mother cat experienced various important events in a synchronistic modality: her anxiety and her inner warning bell, the corresponding mood of her kittens, and the violent storm, although still distant in space and time, in the outside world. If we also assume that a cat's senses are far more acute than our own and that this mother cat must, therefore, have picked up the signals from the environment – possibly smells, vibrations, or changes in the air, the slightest sounds – which we humans cannot perceive, we may say that she also acted within the sphere of chronicity, since she was able to gauge, more or less, how much time she had to save her kittens, and chose the most appropriate action to achieve her goal.

Marco's case: an empathy deficiency

Marco was sent to me when he was about twenty-three by a psychiatric colleague. During our first sessions he told me that for many months he had almost stopped going out, ceased to see friends, given up sport, and been unable to take his exams. He was plagued by terrible anxieties, such as the irrepressible urge to jump off a bridge while walking across it, or out of an open window when he saw one. We could say that his imaginal world had been taken over by what he would one day describe as "dead thoughts."

This young patient had not been able to express his emotions during childhood because his parents, who were afraid of everything they could not foresee or control, would not have acknowledged them. During the analytical exchange we reconstructed that his parents had presented him with an image of himself that had nothing to do with his natural traits, but was rather an ideal image of what he should have been, above all for the purpose of placating their anxieties. Years later, Marco explained to me that he could not experience joy, because it was a feeling that would have distanced him from his parents who were sad; but neither could he experience sadness, anxiety, or any other problematic state of mind, because it would have meant that his parents had failed to perform their function of satisfying his desires and making him happy. If they had realized this, however, they would have been plunged into a state of unresolvable anxiety, which would have distanced them more and more from their boy's world. Since parental recognition is the indispensable premise for the manifestation of a sense of existence, Marco had found himself trapped in a paradoxical double bind: "To exist you must not feel anything, but if you do not feel anything you do not exist." As he so meaningfully put it: "My parents were absent, but their shadow hung over me ..." On another occasion, in the light of important considerations that emerged in analysis, he said: "If the memory of the past, with the shadow it can trigger, is not relived and overcome, then the past invades the present and obscures it."

This story seems to me emblematic of how the lack of a synchronicity experience in infancy, due to the parents' inability to mirror the archaic experiences of the child and to give them back to him through a shared form of representation warmed by affection, makes self-expression and the entrance into historical time impossible. Marco himself explained this very well: "In the beginning it is our parents' acceptance that gives us our points of reference and our time. If you are told: 'You are like this and you must stay like this,' time never begins." Hence, Marco had never been able to configure his past experiences in a communicable experience and he had let his emotions die as he was growing up. When faced with any situation that required his affective involvement he was seized by a panic fear that obliged him to escape, and then to falsify or deny the demands of reality and his own desire: "If I express an emotion, that is who I am, and if I can't do it, or if that emotion doesn't materialize because it is not accepted and recognized, then I am annihilated." To protect his identity that he felt was "like a tiny flame that could have been extinguished by the slightest puff of wind," he had hidden it in what he called "an idea of himself" and it was as if his whole affective sphere and even his corporeal sensibility had atrophied. One day, after a certain period of analysis, he realized that he was beginning to experience sensations again, and confided to me that he had not felt heat or cold for years. He had increasingly reduced his contacts with the outside world and had taken refuge in a deep niche of his being, seeking to live as little as possible: "When you can't say things because they're not understood, you reach a point where you can't think them and, in the end, you can't even feel them." One day he explained to me just how separate he felt from his emotions: "Just feeling a hint of one was enough to trigger an angry reaction. As soon as I was touched by an emotion I rejected it and the rejection became emptiness ... but the rejection lasted a moment and the emptiness for ever."

Thus, by entering into collusion with the pathological mental processes of his parents, Marco created a perfect and unattainable model for himself, which was both what he had to be and what he would never be able to be. A double that, on the one hand, seductively promised him salvation by magically solving all his problems, and, on the other, took the form of a ruthless enemy who stole everything he might have been and condemned him to an insurmountable feeling of inadequacy, to defeat and, indeed, to annihilation. The model's victory presupposed the destruction of everything that was imperfect, and hence Marco's reality in the making, which was boundless yet unfinished, because it was inscribed in space and time.

The fundamental task of the analytical therapy was slowly to reconstruct in Marco's inner world a parental function that was altruistic and empathic towards his child self, as he gradually reactualized it through memory, and also towards the infantile and confused part of his parents, while at the same time developing an attitude of compassion and forgiveness towards them.

I would like to conclude my account of this clinical experience by transcribing the thoughts Marco communicated to me at an advanced stage in the therapy:

> The heroic was the counterweight of destiny. My identity, or at least my image of myself, was caught between two demands and could neither be illuminated nor take form. In replying to the question "Who are you?", which terrified me, I would have thought who I wanted or had to be. I had a sense of emptiness, of failure, of unbearable inadequacy. Whatever I did or said was wrong, whoever I was was wrong. In actual fact, I had to be "another." Identity was like an external proposal that I had to take on. I had to adhere to that proposal like an image attached to a model, but it wasn't me. Now we've given identity another meaning. There's no need for others to give it to me, I have it, I don't necessarily have to possess that absolute knowledge I once thought would free me from all my ills. I don't know everything, yet I can

walk and live. The image has changed: "from being a hero to being myself!" Moreover, real identity is a "tension" towards something. I experience a sense of belonging and, at the same time, openness, which weren't there before ... How worthless was the perfection I strove for, and how rich and, in a certain sense, "infinite" is this limit I shunned!

A clinical experience: synchronicity interrupted

Now I would like to discuss parts of an analysis conducted by one of my colleagues who is a member of the Laboratorio Analitico per Immagini, founded by Paolo Aite. My colleague, whom I would sincerely like to thank for having given me permission to make reference to this patient of hers, uses Sandplay, and she gave a detailed account of this case during a study day at the AIPA. Her patient is a man of around forty who was unable to experience any kind of affective relationship because he adopted a series of strategies to bring about his abandonment, after which he experienced a sense of utter desperation. According to the patient, his inability to maintain a relationship was linked to his body, which he experienced as a place of shame, suffering, and humiliation due to the fact that two phalanges of the little finger of his left hand are missing. In the sand tray he mixed the sand with water to make actual sculptures that represented a mutilated body without arms and the upper part of the head and with the chest marked by fractures, which he described as "disgusting." In another tray he constructed a mountain on which he placed a musical box, saying: "It's the most mechanical thing I found and for me 'mechanism' means that life is horrible, that everything is horrible and that I am horrible." In another tray, he replaced the musical box with a small piano: "Music marks time in an implacable way." This man's drama began at the age of about four, when he was alone in the house one day and went outside to find his mother lying on the lawn in the garden in a state of intoxication: she did not see him and was completely unaware of his presence because, as he reconstructed later, she was completely "stoned." During all his years at school, his mother had always been present and caring in the morning but when he came home – always to find a good meal waiting for him – he would gradually lose her when she started to "smoke" in the afternoon until she was totally on another planet. It was no accident that next to the musical box in the sand tray there was a small cardboard clock, the kind used to teach children to tell time, with the hands at 5 o'clock in the afternoon: the hour when his mother, though physically present, became mentally absent. Therefore we may say that the dimension of chronicity represented a terrible nightmare for this patient, because at a certain point during the time frame of the day, the little boy inexorably lost his mother and, with her, the beginning of a happy synchronic modality of time that had been sketched out in the empathic relationship with her. To make matters worse, he felt that he was under a cloud of shame, because it was inconceivable for a woman to be a "druggie" in a small town like his. The word could not even be mentioned! The last thing the man represented in the sand tray – as described by my colleague – was a boy seen sideways on, with his legs in a running position and his arms in front of him, with his forearms raised and his hands, with all the fingers, close to his face. The patient said that the image represented him when he was four, and made the following comment: "He is 'the little boy in the garden' and he doesn't know if he is running or sleeping." I think this sculpture expresses the two extreme modalities the patient used to protect himself from existential angst: on the one hand, escaping from history and interrupting the contact with the world and with others that places us in measurable temporality, which was a source of suffering for him; on the other, taking refuge in the achronistic temporality of sleep and dreaming, where there is no beginning and no end, no sudden eruption of tragedy. In so doing, he no longer perceived his mother as absent and incapable of seeing him or responding to his demands, needs, and hunger for affective contact.

Since this personal drama is being re-enacted for and shared by the analyst, that is a human being who sees it and listens empathically, we can only hope that, as therapy progresses, the patient will be able to transform that past (*illo tempore*), which is eternal and untouched by history, and, in a certain sense, is already saving him from nothingness, into an actual "story" to insert, in the form of synchronicity, between himself and others, between himself and the world. Only this first and happy synchronicity modality can act as the prelude to his entrance into chronistic temporality.

The Ego-Self dialogue and the assimilation of shame

As you so rightly say, the Ego can reflect on the four temporality modalities of which you speak and include them in a coherent narrative, but it cannot integrate and unify them. This can only be done by a more complex agency than the Ego which you identify as the Ego-Self axis, in line with Jungian thought. In fact, Jung states that the *Ego* is the *center of consciousness*, whereas the Self is the *center* of the total personality, which includes *consciousness*, the *unconscious*, and the *Ego*.

At the level of the collective unconscious, however, psyche is still one with matter; hence the Self is much more than an Ego, simply because it embraces the others, the inner depths of the psyche and the entire world.

The last reflection I would like to make on your paper concerns the repercussions that the dialogue between Ego and Self can have on the feeling of guilt and the consequent sense of shame. As you rightly say, shame can act as a guide within temporality because it makes the human Ego conscious of its finite condition and its limits, as well as its capacity to do good or evil. But perhaps, just as the Ego alone cannot unify the diverse temporality modalities, it cannot integrate the opposites in the broader sense: light and darkness, innocence and guilt, temporal and eternal, male and female, human and divine. Thus, the problem of evil, the reason for its existence in the creation of the world and of our life, risks becoming an unresolvable dilemma. Why was a world without evil not possible? We risk feeling condemned to sin and, instead of increasing our empathic capacity through a feeling of humility, we could remain locked in a reaction of rejection and anger.

But if the Self is rooted in the sphere of absence of chronistic temporality, which, like the mythical place of the Divinity, is an eternal temporality, then it is precisely through the profound contact with the Self that the Ego can experience the sense of evil, and consequently guilt and shame, in a non-destructive way. The Ego will draw on the meaning of history, of the birth of the world and of the dimension of chronistic temporality when, precisely by becoming aware of its limits, it can transcend them through an experience that will open it to the infinite.

If I had to imagine a primordial god, who represented the dimension of the Self on a psychic level, in the act of creating the world and, subsequently, the chronistic temporality of the Self, I would draw inspiration from the images of a dream experienced by a woman at the end of depth psychology therapy. This is the dream:

> A surgeon was performing a delicate operation on a man's brain. He had to connect the "centers of evil" to the peripheral nerve pathways. At a certain point the surgeon hesitated and, seized by a profound anxiety, said to his assistant: "If the operation fails, the man could become a delinquent, a murderer when he regains consciousness: perhaps it would be better to give up and let him die." But the assistant exclaimed loudly: "We must risk it, let's keep going." The dreamer saw that the surgeon's assistant was her analyst.

I think this dream clearly illustrates that the abstract principle of evil (the cerebral "centers of evil") can only become evil that is carried out or acted out and, as history teaches us, cause harm and suffering to all creatures and nature itself, within a dimension of chronistic temporality. On the other hand, if an Ego entity, as the center of the field of individual consciousness, does not detach itself from the original Self, evil remains a mere possibility and, at most, an evil without guilty parties, like that unleashed by animals or natural disasters. In this case, however, not even life could unfold fully because it would be devoid of a consciousness that mirrored it.

Considering the Judeo-Christian myth, we may suppose that not even God was able to violate the laws of reality in creating the universe, and that it could not but be composed of lights and shadows, good and evil, awareness and unawareness. Perhaps a world without evil would have been perfect, but it could never have existed. As Trevi writes, the fundamental philosophical question "*Si Deus est, unde malum?*" could also be reversed: "*Si malum non est, unde Deus?*" (Trevi and Romano 1975, p. 32). In relation to the above dream, we might imagine Divine Wisdom as a female spiritual figure who assisted God when he doubted the goodness of His creation. Out of a love for life, she would have borne the wounds inflicted by all future violence, by all guilt and by all the suffering that would have been experienced, in order to prevent the world from being plunged into gloom without time and without hope.[1]

Note

1   The tale of this dream and comments regarding it appears in my book *Silenzio a Praga* (Caramazza 2017).

Appendix

Correspondence between authors (March 2018)

On 25 March 2018 Murray Stein wrote:

Dear Elena,
    I have read your comments with great interest and am impressed by your profound grasp of the issues regarding temporality and its various modes. It's clear that we live in several temporality at once, and your memories and clinical accounts show this so well. I love the story about the mother cat and your memory of the onset of

chronicity consciousness. When this is ruptured, shame and mistrust enter profoundly into a person's attitude toward self and others.

Regarding the problem of evil, the dream you recount offers a lot to think about. For certain, evil is beyond the grasp and responsibility of the ego, although the ego has a responsibility to be aware of it whenever and to whatever degree it can be. I attach a little paper I wrote comparing Neumann's and Jung's perspectives on the problem of evil. This was given at a conference in Israel a couple of years ago (2015) and published in a book titled *Turbulent Times, Creative Minds.* I wish I had the dream you mention to include in the discussion. By the way, please translate for me Trevi's question and your reply, if you don't mind. I want to be sure I have it right.

Warmly, Murray

On 28 March 2018 Elena Caramazza wrote:

Dear Murray,

I am glad that you liked my comments, which sprang from your poetical paper, from my heart and from my memories. As soon I have read your paper on Evil I will send you my comments together perhaps with a part of my chapter "Shadow" in the *Analytical Psychology Treatise*, edited by Aldo Carotenuto (published in Italian by UTET).

Trevi's question is "If God exists, whence Evil comes? His answer is: "If Evil does not exist, where is God?"

Warmly, Elena

Bibliography

Caramazza, E. (2017) *Silenzio a Praga.* Moretti e Vitali, Bergamo.
Trevi, M. and Romano, A. (1975) *Studi sull'ombra.* Marsilio, Venezia.

Chapter 5

Erich Neumann and C.G. Jung on "the problem of evil"

Murray Stein

The "problem of evil" is indelibly inscribed into the Table of Contents of our collective memory, conscious and unconscious, and this chapter was deeply read and commented upon by both C.G. Jung and Erich Neumann. It is a critical topic not only for theologians, philosophical ethicists, artists (of all kinds), criminologists, and cultural historians, but also, and today perhaps most of all, for psychologists because of the question of human motivation to commit evil acts. Perhaps it was due to the excessively cruel times they lived in that Jung and Neumann focused on this issue in their writings with such laser-like energy. Yet it is also an age-old question that has inspired agonized reflections throughout recorded history: What is evil, whence does it come, and how are we to deal with it? These same questions are no less with us today, although our answers tend to be less mythological than in ancient times and more sociological, philosophical, political, or psychological (Curatorium 1967).

For psychology, the problem of evil brings the issue of ethics front and center. Ethics is a product of human consciousness attempting to confront the problem of evil and to contain it by defining it, setting up boundaries for behavior, proposing horizons and perspectives from a variety of cultural settings, and perhaps setting up some specific rules of behavior. The elaboration of ethics is an on-going human project because times and cultural settings change and evolve, which create new issues to consider. Psychology may be able to contribute some insights into the motivation and the psychic roots of evil as defined by ethical contructs, and it may also offer some suggestions for how to deal with evil on an individual and a social/collective level by considering levels of responsibility for actions deemed to be evil and designing methods of containment, punishment, and conditions of atonement that follow a judgment of evil-doing.

A question for us as depth psychologists is: Can ethics be grounded in psychology as we understand it, or is ethics a matter purely of legal considerations, therefore wholly conscious, culturally conditioned, and relative or even arbitrary? Traditionally, ethics has been embedded in mythological and theological foundations and has been seen as derivative from such things as "the will of God, or the gods." In modernity, this does not wash any longer. We do not live in an age of faith. Yet there is a need for ethics, and the conviction that evil exists continues to occupy us. So can ethics be rooted in psychological perspectives as it once was in mythological and theological ones? This would be a point for discussion between depth psychology on the one side and theology, philosophy, criminology, and other social sciences as well as neurobiology on the other. My attempt at establishing a depth psychological basis for ethics in psychology is represented in *Solar Conscience/Lunar Conscience* (Stein 1993), in which I argue for an archetypal ground for an ethical attitude in two types of innate conscience. In other words, I believe that humans are innately ethical creatures, but not only so: they are also innately given to the opposite, to violations of the laws written in their hearts, and when this force takes charge people become possessed by evil. This is the great theme of Gnosticism and symbolized by the monster god Yaldabaoth (Stein 2014, p. 87). This is a problem of inherent opposites embedded in the human psyche itself, and therefore not resolvable on a rational and purely conscious level try as we might to master the problem of evil.

From a depth psychological viewpoint, the problem of evil is connected to the perception that it is largely controlled by unconscious factors. With the exception of out-and-out psychopaths, evil-doing is something people generally try to avoid, at least to some extent. Most people want to be on the side of the good, or at least seen to be so, not on the side of evil. So the enactment of evil is generally much more subtle and insidious than it is consciously malicious. One may in all good conscience serve evil while consciously intending to do good by obeying an evil law, for instance. Evil operates and may be done in perfect innocence, with good intentions and a sense of civic responsibility. Jesus on the cross praying, "Father, forgive them; for they know not what they do" (Luke 23:34), speaks to this point. Evil's will is carried out unknowingly and with a sense of duty. It is invisible. Evil uses the ego's talents, its will, and its powers, to do its malicious work. The ego rationalizes marvelously and indeed infinitely, convinced by its own deceptions and rhetoric. When the ego serves evil, whose hand in the matter is kept hidden, even the "law," which speaks ostensibly for truth and justice, may itself be used to subvert those very values. The ego is unconsciously complicit in this and puts forward the law to cover the handiwork of evil. This is the problem of evil as seen from the perspective of depth psychology.

Erich Neumann brilliantly describes this psychological problem of consciously identifying with the good and remaining unconscious of the evil within ourselves in his book, *Depth Psychology and a New Ethic*. An individual or a community identifies itself wholly with the good and projects evil outward, he writes, and thus remains free from guilt in consciousness no matter what atrocities might be performed against the perceived "evil other." This is the well-known scapegoat phenomenon (Neumann 1969, pp. 50ff.). Neumann's solution as described in *Depth Psychology and a New Ethic* is for the individual or the community to become aware of the shadow within, to take it fully into account in decision-making and behavior, and to consider all the consequences of subsequent actions for oneself and for others. It is a tall order. The "new ethic" takes the normal ethical position of careful and scrupulous obedience to a moral tradition a step further by making evil conscious as an inner factor and not projecting it exclusively onto the malefactor. This would apply to individuals and collectives (corporations, nations, etc.) alike. It says: Consider your own shadow – your hidden agenda, your most devious motives, your secret desires and inclinations – before you criticize, attack, or condemn the other. This demands the onerous psychological work of recognizing and accepting one's own shadow as a part of one's selfhood, thereby relativizing naive claims to purity and virtuous righteousness. Simply being a victim is not good enough to justify retaliatory shadow enactments and revenge. Before claiming the high ground, he says, consider your own shadowy regions. In fact, psychologically considered, there is no high ground without a low ground right beside it.

Jung's analysis of the problem of evil is somewhat different, although on many points in agreement with Neumann's. After reading Neumann's "New Ethic" and praising it, Jung writes:

> One of the toughest roots of all evil is unconsciousness and I could wish that the saying of Jesus, "Man, if thou knowest what thou doest, thou art blessed, but if thou knowest not, thou art accursed, and a transgressor of the law," were still in the gospels, even though it has only one authentic source. It might well be the motto for a new morality.
>
> (Jung 1948/1969, par. 291)

Here we see Jung advocating with Neumann for a "new morality" based on the same idea of making the unconscious shadow conscious before acting. Jung, however, is skeptical about the human capacity for sustaining such a level of consciousness; moreover, in *Answer to Job* (Jung 1952/1969), his later confrontation with the problem of evil as an archetypal matter, he tells us why even such consciousness of the personal shadow would be insufficient for the absolute solution to the problem of evil. Something more is needed. What would that be?

The background of both Neumann's and Jung's reflections on the problem of evil in the 1930s, 1940s, and 1950s is the grave situation in Europe – the German "schizophrenic episode" as Neumann calls it (Jung and Neumann 2015, p. 140); the collective state of "possession" (*Ergrifenheit*) in Germany by the archaic Germanic god, Wotan, as Jung describes it (Jung 1936/1964, par. 386); the catastrophic aftermath of war and the horrors of the holocaust; the Stalinist atrocities in Russia; and the threat of atomic warfare as the West faced off with the Soviet Union in the Cold War. How to understand this extraordinary rupture in moral consciousness in modern culture and history on a collective level, and how to manage evil on the personal and the collective level – these were the enormous questions that preoccupied them. The proposals they came up with are highly relevant today, too, and will be for as long as humans have to struggle with the problem of evil, which means most likely forever, or as long as human beings as we know ourselves and our psychology continue to exist.

The problem of evil, as we consider it in psychology, results from the problem of opposites built into our very nature. In the course of personality development, the self becomes divided. Ego-consciousness necessarily separates itself out from the original wholeness of the personality as given in the primal self, and it leaves behind in the shadow all the rejected and unacceptable tendencies and everything else that cannot be integrated into this small territory of the psyche that we reference as our personal identity, whether personal or collective. Thus a counter-will takes form in the psychic system: the one side strives in a certain direction, usually toward attachment to others and adaptation to environmental conditions, while the other goes in a very different one, namely toward isolation and naked self-assertion. On one side we are family people and decent citizens, on the other egoistic monsters and criminals. Or vice versa. This is why we have a secret alliance with the opposite other and collude with the shadow enactments of others, sometimes even cheering them on. The more tension one places on the system by emphasizing the positive features of the conscious side over the negative features of the unconscious shadow, the more the split deepens and thus creates neurotic conflicts, increases the strength of defenses such as projection, and exacerbates the differences until the one is all light and the other all dark. This sets up the condition for enactments where evil uses the personal shadow to do its will, all the while remaining hidden and unconscious to the doer. Neumann's thesis is that this problem can be overcome or at least greatly ameliorated by making the shadow conscious and thereby defusing the power of evil. Jung is not so sure. Evil may be beyond human capacities of conscious containment by this means. This is a point of disagreement between them.

In a late letter, dated 3 June 1957, Jung writes to Neumann:

In relation to the so-called *New Ethic* we are basically quite in agreement, but I prefer to express this delicate problem in a rather different language. It is not really a question of a "new" ethic. Evil is and always remains the thing one knows one should not do. Man overestimates himself unfortunately in this respect: he thinks it is within his discretion to intend good or evil. He can persuade himself of this, but in reality he is, in view of the greatness of these opposites, simply too small and too unconscious to be able to choose the one or the other in free will and under all circumstances. It is much more the case that he does or does not do the good that he would like to for overwhelming reasons, and that in the same way, evil just happens to him like misfortune.

(Jung and Neumann 2015, p. 327)

Jung thinks that Neumann is overestimating the capacities of human consciousness in his description of the "new ethic." Evil is so large and so insidious a force that human consciousness is incapable of encompassing it and escaping its manipulations. We must remember that Jung thought of evil as an archetypal and collective power and not only a personal shadow feature of the personality. Evil is a force with a personality like Satan that is transpersonal and vastly superior to the ego's ability to know or understand its insidious ways. Always we are tricked by it into doing that which we would not do, and not doing that which we would do. When speaking of the problem of evil, Jung is thinking of Goethe's Mephisto, of the Antichrist of Christian theology, of Satan in the Book of Job and such archetypal figures and not only or even primarily of the shadow material that is housed in the complexes of the personal unconscious. Evil draws on the power of instinct and archetype and is conceptualized by Jung as an inherent aspect of the self, as a kind of autonomous spiritual force, just as goodness is. They are a pair of opposites resident in the self: Christ and anti-Christ. For Jung, as he writes in *Answer to Job*, human consciousness (represented by the figure of Job) may be an instrument for bringing about a reduction of archetypal evil by instigating a development in the Self (represented by Yahweh), but the transformation must be carried out above the ego's head, so to speak, that is, by the Self in its own progressive unfolding and internal integration process. The problem of evil is just too big for humans to solve by means of their frail conscious powers, as important as consciousness is in instigating evolution in the self. Thus becoming conscious of the shadow and taking it into account in our decisions and actions will not place us beyond enactments of evil. Humans will always be vulnerable to the wiles and power of the evil one. So argues Jung.

Neumann answers Jung's letter a few days later. In his reply, he tells Jung of an experience in active imagination that lay at the source of his work on ethics and the problem of evil.

> *The New Ethic* was the attempt to process a series of phantasies that roughly corresponded time-wise with the exterminations of the Jews, and in which the problem of evil and justice was being tossed around in me. I am still gnawing away at these images at the end of which, in brief, stands the following. I seemed to be commissioned to kill the ape-man in the profound primal hole. As I approached him, he was hanging, by night, sleeping on the cross above the abyss, but his—crooked—single eye was staring into the depths of this abyss. While it at first seemed that I was supposed to blind him, I all of a sudden grasped his "innocence," his dependence on the single *eye of the Godhead* [my italics], which was experiencing the depths through him, which was a human eye. Then, very abridged, I sank down in opposite this single eye, jumped into the abyss, but was caught by the Godhead, which carried me on the "wings of his heart." After that, this single eye opposite the ape-man closed and it opened on my forehead. (Bit difficult to write this, but what should one do.) Working outward from the attempt to process this happening, I arrived at *The New Ethic*. For me, since then, the world looks different. Your formulations in the letter are also valid for me, but they do not go far enough.
>
> (Jung and Neumann 2015, p. 331)

Neumann's moving account of the source of his thinking about the problem of evil and a "new ethic," which emerged in the period of maximum threat to the Jewish people, answers Jung on a level that

seems to go far beyond his more rational theses in *New Ethic*. I sur-
mise that this letter brought a new level of respect to Jung's already
high estimation of his most gifted student, for he writes back to Neumann that he is changing some paragraphs in a paper he was writing
on the problem of conscience at the time (Jung and Neumann 2015,
p. 334). In his account of this active imagination, Neumann reveals his
ultimately decisive degree of faith in God. He is supposed to kill the
ape-man and finds this primitive being (a classic shadow image) staring
into the primal hole, an abyss of evil. The ape-man itself is innocent,
however, as he discovers when he sees him staring down through the
eye of the Godhead, which is at the same time a human eye. God
is using the eye placed in the primitive ape-man to look into the depths
(to become conscious of His own depths). Then the narrator jumps
into the abyss himself! This is a remarkable "leap of faith," as made
famous by Kierkegaard, and as with Abraham, about whom Kierkegaard is writing as the great model for the man of faith, there is a
divine intervention and he is caught and carried on the "wings of his
heart." Neumann says that this experience transformed him and gave
him the confidence he needed to find a solution to the problem of evil:
"For me, since then, the world looks different."

There is in Neumann's writing a kind of rapturous embrace of evil as
though by embracing it he is also embracing God, as though evil is a
part of God and this is a path to being near to God's will:

> [A]s I see it, I do not fall, but jump, and I know that the danger
> exists that I will die, but my prayer goes that "wings of the heart"
> may hold me. This means that I am, in my action, within and not
> outside of the Godhead, because it is not about an action of the
> ego, but about a happening that I must hand myself over to. If the
> issue of "Job" is relevant, according to which the Godhead wishes
> to come to consciousness, an aspect of its subjectivity is evident,
> then I have to live with the single eye of the Godhead and also to
> experience the darkness of the abyss. But then evil is not a sin, but
> part of the world to be experienced.
>
> (Jung and Neumann 2015, p. 332)

The leap is a mystical moment of encounter and realization, and this
ultimately leads to complete acceptance of reality as it unfolds before
us in history. This is Neumann's solution to the problem of evil. Evil is
a part of God, and so paradoxically by participating in history, even if
evil-doing is part of it, humans are participating in God's will. I believe
that when Jung read this he realized that he was dealing with a human

being of profound and bold religious imagination and intuitions quite similar to his own.

Jung had been preoccupied with the problem of evil and ethics from very early on in his professional life. In part, this was due to his friendly but quite sharp exchanges with religious professionals like his Zurich friend, Adolf Keller, the pastor of St. Peter's church in Zurich and a founder of the World Council of Churches (Jehle-Wildberger 2014). Jung was often challenged by his religiously minded colleagues about the ethics of individuation, and he had to formulate a response to this question. It touched upon the question of responsibility, to oneself, to others, and to the social world. Is individuation itself morally defensible? The argument that it is not has been made by some of his critics, such as Martin Buber.

In *Answer to Job*, written in a feverish few months during a mild illness in early 1951, Jung takes up the problem of evil in both a highly personal way but also speaking to and for all of Christendom. He offers a stinging critique of Christianity and its cultural effects in history. Christianity, by one-sidedly supporting and affirming the good ("God is light and in Him there is no darkness") and denying the reality of evil in the pernicious (to Jung) doctrine of evil as *privatio boni* (absence of good) and by relegating Satan to eternal damnation, in the end split good and evil even further apart than it had been heretofore, and this played into the hands of Evil, paradoxically. Identifying itself with the good, Christianity projected evil outward (onto the Jews, among others), just as Neumann describes the old ethic in his *New Ethic* book, and now "after the catastrophe" of World War II and the tragic breakdown of moral fabric in the 20th century it must answer for its dogmatic choices.

To solve the problem of evil in the Christian theological set-up, Jung proposes a further step in the evolution of Christian doctrine and theology – namely, the integration of evil into the Godhead. This would overcome the split and draw evil into a more realistic relationship with the equally archetypal good where dialogue and mutual effects would be possible. This is something already suggested in Neumann's "New Ethic" and strongly advocated in his later letter to Jung in which he describes the origins of his work. Evil must be integrated into the whole. Jung is saying, though, that a process of integration must take place in the pleromatic state, in the Godhead, which could then be reflected in theological dogmas. Dogma does not create the God image of a religion; it reflects it. Mankind can participate in this only to a degree, perhaps like Job stimulating the development through greater consciousness (through the "eye of the Godhead" in a human frame, as shown in Neumann's active imagination).

Is this possible? At the end of his letter to Neumann in 1957, Jung writes:

> I feel myself very uncertain in relation to the question of pessimism and optimism and must leave the solution to fate. The only one who could decide this dilemma, that is dear God himself, has withheld his answer from me so far ...

and then goes on to quote from Candide: "Hopefully you are well *dans ce meilleur des mondes possibles. Tous cela est bien dit, mais il faut cultivar notre jardin*" (Jung and Neumann 2015, pp. 329–30). As ever, Jung is ironical when speaking of God (Neumann had pointed this out to him already when he first read the draft of *Answer to Job*), and so he remained undecided. Unlike Neumann, he was not carried on "the wings of his [i.e., God's] heart."

Will the problem of evil ever be solved? Will good prevail over evil by integrating it into the larger whole? Or will evil prevail by remaining outside the whole and causing endless trouble from this position as outsider to the Godhead? In the end, each of us is left with this question. Neumann seems to cast his ballot on the side of the faithful; Jung seems to remain skeptical, but perhaps hopeful, in a slightly ironic way.

Bibliography

Curatorium of C.G. Jung Institute (Ed.). (1967). *Evil*. R. Manheim and H. Nagel (trs). Evanston, IL: Northwestern University Press.

Jehle-Wildberger, M. (2014). *C.G. Jung und Adolf Keller*. Zurich: Theologischer Verlag.

Jung, C.G. (1936/1964). Wotan. In *Collected Works* 10, paras. 371–399. Princeton, NJ: Princeton University Press.

Jung, C.G. (1948/1969). A psychological approach to the dogma of the Trinity. In *Collected Works* 11, paras. 169–295. Princeton: Princeton University Press.

Jung, C.G. (1952/1969). Answer to Job. In *Collected Works* 11, paras. 553–758. Princeton: Princeton University Press.

Jung, C.G. and Neumann, E. (2015). *Analytical Psychology in Exile: The Correspondence between C.G. Jung and Erich Neumann*. M. Liebscher (ed.) and H. McCartney (tr.). Princeton, NJ: Princeton University Press.

Neumann, E. (1969). *Depth Psychology and a New Ethic*. E. Rolfe (tr.). New York: G.P. Putnam's Sons.

Stein, M. (1993). *Solar Conscience/Lunar Conscience*. Wilmette, IL: Chiron Publications.

Stein, M. (2014). *Minding the Self: Jungian Meditations on Contemporary Spirituality*. London and New York: Routledge.

Chapter 6

The problem of evil

Elena Caramazza

Thank you, Murray, your writings always give me so much food for thought.

In particular, I am fascinated by Jung's consideration – in certain respects divergent from Neumann's thought – that Ego consciousness alone does not have the capacity to contain the problem of evil, nor the power to solve it. It is not enough to illuminate one's Shadow so that it will no longer be prey to the mechanism of repression that inevitably leads to the projection of all evil onto an enemy to be fought and defeated. Nor is it enough to abandon the most robust defenses against the Shadow, such as denial or splitting. When it comes to evil the greatest value of the birth of consciousness, understood as the capacity to formulate an ethical judgment, may be its ability to trigger a process of transformation that extends to the entire Self, thus involving our biological and archetypal substratum.

For Jung, in fact, the metaphysical and psychological aspects of evil are inseparable because God and archetype of the Self are indistinguishable and – since all reality is experienced through images – the representation of God and of the Self correspond: the soul is to God what the eye is to light. Significant in this respect is the following passage: "man's achievement of consciousness appears as the result of prefigurative archetypal processes or – to put it metaphysically – as part of the divine life process. In other words, God becomes manifest in the human act of reflection" (Jung 1942–8/1958, p. 161).

We may also say that if evil had never existed redemption, or atonement for guilt, would never have been possible. At a psychological level, perhaps, this means reuniting evil with its opposite, good, and suffering the clash between them in one's own soul. This way the conflict would not be expelled or resolved by excluding one or the other, but assimilated *in toto* by the inner self, which, like an alchemical vessel, would induce a reaction between the different elements, and the birth of a new substance. Hence, redeeming evil does not mean van-quishing or destroying it, but assimilating and willingly and con-sciously accepting the fact that we will be transformed by the clash between the opposing factors. Perhaps it is only through such a courageous psychic act that evil, too, will undergo a transformation, along with our "so-called" good!

Panikkar often spoke of the god Shiva, who in various representa-tions is depicted in blue because he has swallowed all the poison of the world in order to neutralize it by digesting it and synthesizing it in a new, harmless substance. We who are not gods but limited human beings can only absorb the small part of evil that we can tolerate and modify. In *Aion* Jung states: "it is quite within the bounds of possibility for a man to recognize the relative evil of his nature, but it is a rare and shattering experience for him to gaze into the face of absolute evil," understood as all existing evil (Jung 1951/1968, p. 10). Nonetheless, since the psyche is not only Ego but also Self, and contains "collective man" who participates in the destiny of all humanity, we are also able to feel that we are a link in the human chain working to achieve the global redemption of evil: a task rooted in the archetypal dimension of the Divine.[1]

Apropos of how we might conceive the interaction between a divine figure who created the world, the birth of consciousness and the chal-lenging problem of evil, I would like to quote from my latest book *Silenzio a Praga* an extract in which I compare the Judeo-Christian myth with an Indian myth recounted by Panikkar, since I think it might interest you.

Regards, Elena Caramazza

From *Silenzio a Praga*

For Jung, the God of the Judeo-Christian tradition is unconscious of his deep-seated antinomy and, possibly to reassure himself that he exists and has certain values, he demands that man acknowledge his power and extol him, especially for his sense of justice.

> From the way the divine nature expresses itself we can see that the individual qualities are not adequately related to one another, with the result that they fall apart into mutually contradictory acts. For instance, Yahweh regrets having created human beings, although in his omniscience he must have known all along what would happen to them.
>
> (English 1958, p. 372. Italian: 1952/1979, p. 350)

Jung also states that Yahweh's character

> fits a personality who can only convince himself that he exists
> through his relation to an object. Such dependence on the object is
> absolute when the subject is totally lacking in self-reflection and
> therefore has no insight into himself. It is as if he existed only by
> reason of the fact that he has an object which assures him that he
> is really there. [...] Existence is only real when it is conscious to
> somebody. That is why the Creator needs conscious man even
> though, from sheer unconsciousness, he would like to prevent him
> from becoming conscious.
>
> (1958, 372–373. Italian: 1952/1979, p. 350–1)

We may suppose, therefore, that the Creation would not have been
complete without the appearance of man, possessed of consciousness
and hence able to illuminate the dark and contradictory face of the
primitive God. Only at this point would the unconscious ambivalence
of our personal and archetypal original state become a consciously
experienced conflict that could be overcome. Job's desperate questions
concerning the evils wrought upon him would lead God to complete
the Creation by becoming a man in his turn and achieving the consciousness offered to him previously by Job through his ability to
reflect. God answered Job by becoming incarnate. Thus the divine and
human, the unconscious and conscious, the origin and evolution of the
entire cosmos, were reunited.

Concerning the problem of evil – as I wrote some years ago in a
volume on the Shadow (Caramazza 1992, pp. 170–1) – if a god is able
to inflict the worst calamities on man, he still possesses an unconscious
and amoral side on which he has not reflected: ethical action pre-
supposes consciousness. The possibilities are two: either God foresaw
the consequences of his acts and thus had to come to terms with his
injustice, or he used the faculty of omnipotence, forgetting that of
omniscience, and had to come to terms with his blindness. "L'imma-
gine di Dio si scinde per Giobbe ed egli diventa consapevole dell'am-
bivalenza divina" (For Job, the God-image split and he became
conscious of the divine ambivalence) (Jung 1948/1975, p. 118). When
he discovers God's Shadow, Job does not succumb to the hubris of
consciousness because he intuits that the Shadow, with its multiple
aspects of ignorance, primitiveness, and evil, occupies an important
place in the cosmos, even though it remains obscure to reason. Faced
with the temptation of abandoning an incomprehensible God and setting himself up as the sole judge on earth, Job's deeply religious spirit

recognizes its limits and chooses to prostrate itself and worship the Mystery:

> Who is he that hideth counsel without knowledge?
> therefore have I uttered that I understood not;
> things too wonderful for me, which I knew not.
> Hear, I beseech thee, and I will speak:
> I will demand of thee,
> and declare thou unto me.
> I have heard of thee by the hearing of the ear:
> but now mine eye seeth thee.
> Wherefore I abhor myself,
> and repent in dust and ashes.
>
> (Job 42: 3–6)

In acting thus Job is able to avoid the two grave dangers threatening him from above and below: that of refusing to use the tool of judgment and that of identifying with ethical reason. In the first case, he would have doubted his innocence and betrayed his human truth, his guilt feelings would have destroyed him physically and psychically, and nothing new would have happened in the world (in fact, the collective voice insinuated that as God was unquestionably good, the tragedies that had befallen Job could only have been brought about by his having sinned). In the second case, he would have been suspended in a sterile, rarefied limbo, devoid of that vital contact with the sphere of the emotions and the irrational.

If life stimulates consciousness through its chaotic madness, consciousness stimulates life by demanding coherence and sense: "Dio è costretto a ricorrere al peccato dell'uomo: di sapere ciò che è bene e ciò che è male, per il suo scopo di salvazione" (God is obliged to have recourse to human sin: to know what is good and what is evil, for his purpose of salvation) (Jung 1948/1975, p. 165).

The *Deus absconditus* of nature gives Job a terrible lesson but, in his turn, he teaches God justice and compassion.

A comparison between the myth of Yahweh in the Old Testament and the Indian myth of Prajapati, as told in the Brihadaranyaka Upanishad, enables us to see the great event of the Creation of the world by the god of the origins in a different light: Prajapati does not create because he is omnipotent but because in his solitude as the "One" and "Absolute" he is engulfed by sadness, and wishes to experience the joy that can only come from a relationship with the other. Since nothing exists outside him, he is obliged to create from himself. From the dismemberment of his body all the elements of the universe, living beings and human beings are born, and even evil, because through the creation of the *Asuras*, malevolent spirits, darkness becomes manifest (Panikkar 1979/2000, pp. 87–8). We might also say that we are the Divinity's guilt, since the actions of Prajapati are a kind of affront or challenge to the absolute. From this perspective, the original guilt of the Judeo-Christian myth becomes an *originating guilt*. The second act of the divine-human drama – equivalent, perhaps, to the Christian moment of redemption – consists in the creatures offering succour to the dying God when, seized by fear, he invokes them. Hence all the creatures of the world abandon the fascinating mirage of their radical independence and are reunited with their origin, reconstituting the dismembered body of the God. Thus man, accompanied by his whole world but finding himself still to be contingent and therefore eternally itinerant, understands that contingency is not the only dimension of his being, since he is constitutively linked to his divine root. If the essential relationship of reciprocal belonging that enables them to exist to the full were interrupted, God and man might truly lose each other and sink into the abyss of nothingness. For Panikkar the real sin, the real evil is stopping midway on one's existential journey without continuing to the very end.

> Sin is temporality regarded as substance. Existence (ex-sistence) would actually be a fault, a sin even, if it were considered and accepted simply as "sistence", separate from its source and its destiny; none other than a fall – into nothingness. Guilty ignorance (*avidya*) consists in considering ourselves as something independent, substantiating our own self …
>
> (Panikkar 1979/2000, p. 98)

Note

1 Some sentences of this letter come from the chapter: *L'Ombra* (Caramazza 1992).

Bibliography

Caramazza, E. (2017) *Silenzio a Praga*. Moretti e Vitali, Bergamo.
Jung, C. G. (1942–48/1958) A Psychological Approach to the Dogma of the Trinity, in *The Collected Works of C. G. Jung*, vol. XI, *Psychology and Religion: West and East*, Eng. trans. R. F. C. Hull, Pantheon Books Inc., New York. In Italian: Saggio d'interpretazione psicologica del dogma della Trinità, in *Opere*, vol. XI, *Psicologia e Religione*, Boringhieri, Torino (1979).

Jung, C.G. (1948/1975) Symbolik des Geistes. Studien uber psychischen Pha-
nomenologie, tr. It. *La simbolica dello Spirito. Studi sulla Fenomenologia
dello Spirito*, Einaudi, Torino.

Jung C.G. (1951/1968) Aion – Researches into the Phenomenology of the Self,
in *The Collected Works of C. G. Jung*, vol. IX, Part II, Eng. trans R. F. C.
Hull, Princeton University Press, Princeton, NJ. In Italian: Aion – Ricerche
sul simbolismo del Sé, in *Opere*, vol. IX, tomo II, Boringhieri, Torino
(1982).

Jung, C.G. (1952/1979) Antwort auf Hiob, tr. It. *Risposta a Giobbe*, in *Opere*,
vol. XI, *Psicologia e Religione*, Boringhieri, Torino. In English: Answer to
Job, in *The Collected Works of C. G. Jung*, vol. XI, *Psychology and Religion: West and East*, Eng. trans. R. F. C. Hull, Pantheon Books Inc., New
York (1958).

Panikkar, R. (1979/2000) *Mito, Fede ed Ermeneutica. Il triplice velo della
realtà*, Jaka Book, Milano.

Afterword

Fulvia De Benedittis, Sandra Fersurella and Silvia Presciuttini

The fruitful exchange between the two analysts stemmed from a marked convergence of interests, as Caramazza herself points out, and complex themes such as temporality, shame, and the problem of evil are analyzed profoundly from an original and multifaceted perspective. Indeed, we found the correspondence so stimulating and fascinating that it led us to consider the themes addressed in relation to the love relationship and analytic couple therapy, which are the focus of our theoretical/clinical research as Jungian therapists.

The first topic we felt the need to explore was the four modalities of temporality formulated by Stein: in a love relationship, in fact, different temporal phases and experiences occur that seem pervaded by a strong sense of reciprocal communion or by shame and/or guilt.

An overview of Murray Stein's four modalities of temporality

The first of the two polarity pairs of temporality modalities described by Stein is *achronicity-chronicity*, which occupies the horizontal axis in Figure 3.1 (Chapter 3, p. 20). This axis concerns *chronological time*, which is the prerogative of consciousness and of its discriminatory capacities, but also of memory, which processes and connects events in an historical and continuous time. Here the author is referring to a psychic time that is objective and socially shared: a time pervaded and marked by natural events, which is governed by the principal of causality.

All the variations on this axis correspond to modifications of the states of consciousness and of mnemonic capacities. Thus we can have a maximum degree of *achronicity* (point 0) in cases in which consciousness is presumably as yet unformed, as in fetal life; in cases of total unconsciousness due to serious alterations in consciousness, and those in which memory has completely lost its archival and ordering function, as in acute dementia. When in the achronicity mode we are in an atemporal dimension, in the realm of "timelessness and outside of time frames" (Stein, Chapter 3, p. 20).

As an atemporal dimension, *achronicity* does not only concern human consciousness in the universe, but also zero time, before the beginning of universal history. In a similar, and perhaps complementary, way *achronicity* is typical of myth which, characterized by an "iconic constancy" of content, as Blumenberg writes (cited by Stein, Chapter 3, p. 23), becomes a transversal and continuous thread that can interweave, like a constant metanarrative, with chronological, historical time. Myth pertains to the world of the archetypes and to their eternity. Hence, we might say that *achronicity* pertains to the "non-time" of the unconscious, both individual and collective, and also to the "non-time" that existed prior to the Creation.

At the other end of the horizontal axis lies *chronicity* (point 1), which corresponds to the maximum lucidity and discriminatory capacity of consciousness and of the mnemonic function. At point 1, time is marked by facts and well ordered: we are oriented in time and able to distinguish present, past, and future, and to date events with a certain accuracy, if necessary. More often, though, we find ourselves at a point on the line from 0 to 1, rather than at one end or the other. In fact, the individual can experience chronological time in different gradations and modalities, which reflect the actual degree of consciousness and available mnemonic capacity, but also in relation and complementary to the degree of unconscious activity. This happens, for example, in mystic or creative states, day-dreaming, active imagination, and the various phases of sleep. In all these states, consciousness partially gives way to the unconscious in diverse modalities and gradations, thus determining mixed and complementary states of greater or less *achronicity/chronicity* in the individual's experience of time.

The second polarity pair of modalities of temporality described by Stein is *synchronicity-dyschronicity*, which occupies the vertical axis of Figure 3.1 (Stein, Chapter 3, p. 20). Here the author's thought becomes more complex and challenging. In delineating the vertical axis, Stein no longer seems to be referring to the quantity of chronological time, which more or less proceeds from 0 to 1 in the individual's experience, but to a qualitative criterion for evaluating the relationship between achronicity and chronicity in the psyche. Hence, while the horizontal axis of the schema seems more oriented towards a quantitative evaluation of achronicity and chronicity – in the sense of the degree to which one prevails over the other in the psyche – the vertical axis appears to evaluate their reciprocal relationship; for example, whether said temporalities are parallel or whether they converge or diverge in the individual's psyche. The quality of such a relationship constellated in the psyche, will determine the *syn-chronistic* or *dys-chronistic* quality of the individual's temporal experience.

In the *dyschronicity* mode, which Stein describes as the "usual neurotic condition" (Stein, Chapter 3, p. 32), the chronicity (consciousness) and achronicity (unconscious) modalities of temporality form a "disconnected parallel sequence" (Ibid.) in the psyche. This creates discrepancies, contradictions, and blockages in the individual's temporal experience as a whole. In other words, the individual perceives more than one temporality, which coexist but diverge from each other. This dissociation can remain unconscious, creating diverse and incomprehensible temporal senses of the self, or it can be brought to consciousness through a conscious conflict. In the dyschronicity mode, the two temporal modalities of the conscious and unconscious are juxtaposed and experienced separately at a psychic level. Stein places them in a 1+1 relationship.

In the *synchronicity* mode, the individual's experience of time is the completely opposite. Here, the temporal lines of the unconscious and consciousness, desire and the satisfaction of desire, subjective and objective, the intrapsychic and, we might also say, the "supra-psychic," converge unexpectedly and simultaneously in the individual's experience of time and one is multiplied in the other, squaring the value of each. Stein indicates synchronistic temporality as 1 x 1, that is 1 squared.

We believe that synchronicity corresponds to the temporal dimension typical of experiences of *coniunctio* (conjunction) in the alchemical sense: namely, those experiences of childhood, and also adulthood, in which the tendency towards fusion between individual and object and individual and the world prevails. In his description of synchronicity, Stein dwells on the mother-infant relationship, on the syntony that is necessary for the child's desire to be satisfied immediately by the mother, and on the quality of mirroring and communion between the two as they gaze into each other's faces. Reflecting on this, Caramazza wonders if these precocious experiences of synchronicity between mother and child might not act as a bridge between the two temporalities of achronicity and chronicity; if these experiences, concentrated and repeated over time, might not increasingly facilitate the transition from achronicity to chronicity. If this were the case, it would help us to avoid being "trapped" in the achronicity of the unconscious, thus enabling us to restore to consciousness its "hidden treasures and profound mysteries" (Caramazza, Chapter 4, p. 46).

Adults have similar experiences of *coniunctio*, especially in the various states of infatuation, when each partner plays for the other a phantasmic role of mirroring, like the one performed by the primary figure of attachment. However, with the establishment of adulthood and the boundaries of the Ego and consciousness, *synchronicity* ceases to be an ordinary time of the psyche and becomes an *extraordinary time*, an instantaneous and paradoxical event in which a *meaningful coincidence* occurs, though still rarely, between individual and world and conscious and unconscious. In elaborating on his comment on the extraordinary active imagination documented in "The Piano Lesson" by Pauli, Stein delineates two possible schema of the four temporalities he has already described. In the first (Stein, Chapter 3, p. 37) we find in the center "Ego Consciousness," capable of registering the different temporalities present in the psyche, but not of articulating and integrating them in a fluid temporal *continuum*.

In the second schema (Ibid., p. 38), Stein places in the center "The Ring i," the symbol that appears at the end of "The Piano Lesson," which means, as the author emphasizes, that the Ego is no longer at the center of consciousness but has been replaced by the Ego-Self axis.

According to Jung, in fact, conscious and unconscious can integrate *meaningfully* by forming the symbol, via what he calls the *transcendent function*. This function, which brings about the union of opposites and the integration of conscious and unconscious, is not only the work of the Ego, but rather the outcome of a relationship, a system that is constituted between the Ego and the Self, which Jung considered the two fundamental psychic aspects, during the entire individuation process.

Temporality modalities in couples

The four temporality modalities described by Stein also occur in the love relationship, a vital field in which both causality and synchronicity are manifest.

As Marie-Louise von Franz states in one of her texts (1978), the idea of irreversibility in a linear flow of time is inspired by the principle of causality that prevails in Newtonian modern physics, a view that implies a casuistic and linear reading also of psychological events. But Newtonian explanation leaves something to be desired, due to the complexity of psychic life.

Here we shall examine the couple relationship, starting from the stage of falling in love. This can be described as a series of sensations, emotions, fantasies, dreams, and feelings, which totally involve the psyche of the individual. The pre-existing equilibrium between consciousness and unconscious is modified, through an *abaissement du niveau mental*, or lowering of the level of consciousness.

The new and unknown bursts in, yet at the same time there is a sense of something expected and familiar. The person in love finds in the other surprising affinities with psychic parts of themself; he or she discovers strange coincidences in their meeting, which often assume the nature of "signs," destabilizing consciousness; for example, one male patient excitedly described some *meaningful coincidences* that happened during the early stages of courtship and falling in love, when he was forming an emotional attachment to his future wife. Coincidences involving names, birth dates, minor but important interests, and even the way they met – which, on the one hand, seemed quite accidental and unexpected, but on the other, so significant as to seem almost preordained.

In fact, we seem to detect in the psychic dynamics of falling in love the sudden, abrupt transition from the temporality modality of chronicity to that of synchronicity, as described by Stein. The individual who had experienced a "normal sense of a past-present-future continuum in the waking state" (Stein, Chapter 3, p. 20) until the day before, plunges into the synchronicity modality, created by the "surprising and unexpected but meaningful convergence of chronological sequences between ... the inner world of psyche and the outer world of material objects" (Ibid., pp. 22). The more intense and perturbing the love encounter, the more it assumes the characteristics of a synchronistic experience.

In his text on marriage, Jung states that the establishment of a true *psychological relationship* implies emerging from the "unconscious condition of a primitive identity of the ego with others" (Jung 1925, p. xxx). For infatuation to be transformed into a more mature kind of love, as many couple therapists have stressed, reciprocal fantasies and illusions must make room for a certain amount of realism, so that the discriminatory capacity of consciousness may be reacquired in the chronicity mode.

However, the relational life of some couples does not always evolve in this direction once infatuation has ended; instead, it is marked by a stagnant fusion and lack of differentiation. This fusion makes the partners feel as if they are one, and the *dyadic membrane* (Dicks 1967) that separates the inner from the outer in the couple is no longer elastic, but rigid and taut, in defensive opposition to the world.

Stein's concept is also invaluable for understanding the dynamics of a fusional couple, in which the two individuals seem to be stuck in the *achronicity* modality, in a limbo outside the world and time, in an endless present devoid of change and evolution. This relational modality is pathological and anti-evolutionary.

In other couples, instead, a highly conflictual relationship is created, with powerful *dyschronistic* valences in the field. As Jung reminds us, the evolution towards a real psychological relationship requires the development of greater individual consciousness, but this rarely happens without crisis and suffering (Jung 1925).

This brings us to the *Shadow*, the part of the personality that limits the awareness that each partner has of themself, while at the same time hindering the development of the relationship with the other. When infatuated, the partners can share an illusion, in the sense that the other person and some aspects of self are idealized and seen as having no Shadow, while the negative aspects are projected onto the outside world. Thus, the appearance of previously denied content linked to the personal Shadow of either one of the partners can spark a crisis in the couple.

In many of his works, Jung associates the Shadow with the *dark* side of the personality, which comprises not only "negative" characteristics but also content that cannot be assimilated into consciousness (Jung 1917/43), and should be recognized as one's own in the course of development, because it belongs to the profound essence of the personality. The idea of "making the unconscious shadow conscious" which, as Stein writes, is a fundamental ethical problem for the individual, is also central to the maturation of the couple. The integration of the Shadow is, however, an ongoing process; it is never completed, never definitive.

Moreover, the individuative development of each partner takes place on their own time; hence the partners may not be able to confront the Shadow at the same time. In this case, we might say that the couple is in the *dyschronicity* mode. The emergence of Shadow contents leads the couple to confront *guilt* and *shame* in particular; for example, when a betrayal takes place. As Caramazza tells us "shame can act as a guide within temporality because it makes the human Ego conscious of its finite condition and its limits" (Caramazza, Chapter 4, p. 53). In both individual analysis and couple therapy, the confrontation with the Shadow can be activated by the feeling of guilt and by shame. In this way, a new dialogue can be established between the partners, and a new attempt made to integrate opposing content and dyschronistic times. But this does not always happen, and sometimes the partners choose to undertake their individuation process separately.

Guilt and shame: a couple relationship

Achronicity, chronicity, synchronicity, and dyschronicity affect our consciousness in different percentages during the various periods of our life. These temporality modalities interweave like weft and warp to create our most important relationships, which they often tinge with feelings of *shame* and *guilt*.

Let us consider, for example, a case of couple therapy that did not work out, which one of us followed. Claudia and Andrea entered therapy to try and understand what they should do about their relationship. They felt that they were at a point of stalemate and were neither able to stay together nor remain apart. Claudia is very religious and rigidly upholds the values of marriage and family. Andrea confessed that he was seeing another woman and said that he loved Claudia like a sister, but nothing more. We could say, on the basis of Caramazza's and Stein's concepts that, in the achronicity and chronicity continuum, Claudia's life was mainly immersed in achronicity, while Andrea lived, for the most part, in dyschronistic temporality. Claudia experienced an achronistic modality by rigorously adhering to "religious laws and mandates that strictly forbid entertaining certain thoughts or feelings" (Stein, Chapter 3, p. 25). As soon as the subject of a possible separation arose, she seemed pervaded by a sense of *shame*, a vague feeling that appeared to be connected with the devastating collapse of her image and experience of self. Andrea, on the contrary, existed mainly in the dyschronicity mode of the man who refuses to age: a "fitness freak" with a younger lover, who feels *guilty* because he is being unfaithful.

In the first year of therapy, Claudia recounted this dream: *She had to go and pick up a young boy on her Vespa and was late because she couldn't find his helmet.* She then said that this image reminded her of a recurring dream she had as a child that she was not able to finish the things she started. Considering his wife's dream, Andrea associated Claudia's delay in collecting the boy with the fact that she had not yet told their children that the two of them were in couple therapy. Since he and Claudia had not gone out together for some time, Andrea felt obliged to justify himself to the children by telling them that he needed Claudia to accompany him on some errands. However, this image of being needy made him feel ashamed. His father was a strong man who had always sought to satisfy the needs of the whole family, and he felt that he resembled his father in this. What a pity then, commented Claudia, that Andrea's father was accused of sexually abusing his nieces! The family decided not to believe them, saying that they were "mad." Andrea's existing in a dyschronistic temporality seemed to have originated way back: like his father, he found himself experiencing temporal sequences "simultaneously but not as convergent" (Stein, Chapter 3, p. 22). In fact, just as his father did everything to satisfy the family's needs while at the same time abusing his nieces, Andrea was full of affection for the family while cheating on his wife. Andrea also experienced *shame*, which was an expression of his inability to deal with the split between inner and outer, "inherited" from the paternal model. The shameful wound is linked to events, such as betrayal, which create a rift in the image of oneself and in the modulation of self-esteem.

In the "folded and crumpled handkerchief" (Hinton 1999, p. 365, quoted by Stein, Chapter 3, p. 19) of temporality, Andrea saw the image of a strong and caring father, but one stained by shadows of abuse. Moreover, the father had given priority to taking care of Andrea's mother, who had always remained a needy little girl and was thus never able to create a syntony with Andrea.

Also in Claudia's case, the syntony with her mother was pre-cociously interrupted by the arrival of her sick and forbidding grand-mother on her father's side, who had to be taken into their house on principle. We might therefore say, quoting Caramazza, that "when the syntony between mother and infant (and hence between psyche and world) is prevented or brusquely interrupted, the ensuing feeling of shame does not lead to an awareness of blame, of error, or of a sense of responsibility for our actions and their consequences" (Caramazza, Chapter 4, pp. 46–47). The overriding sense of *shame*, experienced as a "pervasive sense of unworthiness, inadequacy" (Ibid., p. 47), had prevented both partners from feeling that they had the right to com-municate their needs and desires to each other. Neither of them had ever reached the point where they could discuss and reconcile their reciprocal needs, and so they drifted apart.

Following Caramazza's line of thought, we might say that this couple was not able to relive and go beyond the memory of the past, which thus invaded the present and definitively obscured their love bond. Claudia's dream images and her desire to finish what she had begun seemed to indicate a desire to shift her epicenter from achroni-city to chronicity, that is towards a way of perceiving time as a past-present-future continuum. Andrea's wanting soon to tell their children that he and Claudia were in therapy also showed that he had a desire to re-immerse himself in the chronicity mode.

The dream that he recounted soon afterwards, appeared to confirm that hypothesis: *A nurse puts a new-born baby into my arms. I know it's not my child and that it has been swapped for another, but I do not attempt to get my own baby back.* Andrea said that he no longer wanted his marriage because he felt he had been too neglected by his wife, who was always dedicated to her work and the home. He knew that their love relationship was finished for ever, but also that this made him feel ashamed and guilty.

It is not easy, in psychoanalysis, to separate the affect of shame from guilt feelings.

While it is true that *shame* is generally associated with mortification, with not being able to live up to the image one has of oneself, guilt is associated with transgression, although the nature of each affect is not that clearly defined (Ballerini and Rossi Monti 1990). *Guilt* feelings can be linked to shame, as in Andrea's case, and sometimes transgression/guilt can be more tolerable than shameful impotence – as in the case of Claudia, caught between religious dictates and betrayal.

In therapy, *guilt* feelings are certainly easier to fathom than the affect of *shame. Shame* is closely related to narcissism and with weakness of the self (Kohut 1971): when conscious, shame is difficult to verbalize because it amplifies unacceptable aspects of self; when unconscious, it is protected by rigid defenses that prevent it from being communicated (Munari and La Scala 1995, 2003).

In the couple sessions held during the first year, the therapist worked on reciprocal blame. Both partners were obliged to face the fact that in the chronicity temporality of their relationship, that is time marked by the clock, they had given increasingly less importance to their love life until, lashed by the winds of individualism, it withered and died. Claudia thought only about work, the children, and finding escape in her beloved novels. Andrea felt neglected and sought attention and warmth elsewhere. Andrea accused his wife of taking no interest in him and Claudia made him feel guilty for betraying her.

They both experienced strong *guilt* feelings, but these were *persecutory feelings of guilt*, where one partner denounces, simply through their presence, the shortcomings of the other and makes them feel in the wrong.

As yet, neither of the two had access to *reparative guilt feelings*: they both lacked the ability to assume the responsibility of understanding why their relationship was over. Neither of the partners was able to work through their individual experiences and their ambivalent feelings about the other. They were both incapable of dealing with the pain of depression.

In the second year of therapy, the occurrence of certain synchronistic events helped the couple to re-enter the shareable chronistic modality of temporality to a greater degree. It happened that Claudia and Andrea invited the Rossis, who had always been their best friends, to dinner to celebrate their daughter's graduation. The daughter had asked the couple for a particular electronic device as a gift. Claudia was curious to see this device and when she went to the shop to look at it, who should she find there but Andrea and Mrs. Rossi, buying it together! During the dinner, Mr. Rossi made strange allusions to the fact that Andrea and his wife were possibly having an affair. Andrea dismissed his suspicions by saying that he was "mad." The next morning Mrs. Rossi offered to drive Claudia to work because her car had broken down. To her amazement and chagrin, Claudia recognized on the dashboard a pen that she herself had given to her husband. She had no more doubts: Mrs. Rossi was Andrea's mistress. Everything came to a head and, after this callous, double betrayal, Claudia decided on a separation. Her *shame* became anger because "the fact that the shame cannot be worked through leaves room for only one possibility: its magical annulment and conversion into anger" (Ballerini and Rossi Monti 1990, p. 125). Hence the manifestation of *anger*, expressed as the need to avenge the wrong suffered, defends the self from shame. Andrea, on the other hand, experienced an increasingly overpowering and embarrassing feeling of shame, which led him to withdraw socially, to avoid being looked at as an unfaithful spouse, and seeing the face of whoever was looking at him.

Andrea and Claudia continued the therapy to arrive at a "civil separation," which was not experienced merely as a painful severance, but as an inevitable journey to meaning that opens up new horizons. Now it was necessary for the Ego to vacate the center of each partner's psyche, which it had occupied so far in their relationship. The Ego had registered the different temporalities present in diverse proportions in the psyche, but had not been able to place them in a tension of opposites filled with meaning. This could only be done if *guilt* and *shame* were worked through by integrating the four modalities of time through the symbol.

Each partner had to arrive at the point where they could embrace generations past and present, as well as relational dynamics of then and now. In short, the Ego had to give way to the Self.

Temporality, coniunctio, and the formation of the symbol in couple therapy.

When commenting on Pauli's active imagination Stein introduces the Axiom of Maria, reprised by Jung from alchemy, which describes the progression of the *coniunctio:* "Out of the one comes the two; out of the two comes the three; and out of the three comes the one as the fourth." Stein stresses its importance by referring to the last chord of four notes, *C E G C*, that Pauli hears as he walks away from the completed "piano lesson" (Stein, Chapter 1, p. 11). This chord signals the appearance of *four* in Pauli's imaginative experience, but, above all, of the symbol as a transformative element and, according to Jung, a unifier of opposites, of the conscious and unconscious.

The progression of the *coniunctio*, from one to four, is a typical characteristic of any deep affective relationship, as Schwartz-Salant has made quite evident in his text *La Relazione* (1998). The *coniunctio* oscillates continuously between a state of union and schism, which is repeated cyclically and involves both partners countless times. In fact, every intense and mature relationship seems to be characterized by a rhythm and dynamics of the field that go from one, to two, to three, and four, in a rapid succession of cycles and temporalities that are experienced by the partners throughout the relationship.

We also see this progression of the *coniunctio* in analytic couple therapy. The first sessions are characterized by a state of chaos in which reciprocal projective identifications and mutual accusations prevail. There is a high degree of unconsciousness in the relationship and the *third area* that is being constituted in the analytic field is undifferentiated and chaotic: a single dense and heavy magma that envelops both the partners and the therapist. In this first state of fusion, which we may consider as *One*, the temporal experience seems to stop and dilate beyond measure, giving rise to a strong feeling of stasis. Therapist and partners find it difficult to date events and place them in a coherent chronological narrative. At the beginning of infatuation, and often at the start of analytic treatment, one senses a powerful experience of *achronicity* in the field, due to the prevalence of unconscious projections. Qualitatively speaking, there is also a sense of *synchronicity*, because the partners often tend not to distinguish between projection and reality, desire and satisfaction of desire, inner and outer world.

During the subsequent period of treatment, the initial magma acquires more of a shape and *Two* is delineated.

Each partner now seems to "act out" in the field a characteristic that is opposite and complementary to the one of the other; the conflict appears more well defined and characterized. For example, during a session one partner may talk a lot and the other remain silent at length; one may be active, the other passive; or one may assume a role that is "rational and lucid," and the other defend their "irrational and creative" attitude. During this phase the schism, the struggle between opposites, prevails and the analyst is drawn now towards one partner, now towards the other. Many pairs of opposites can be constellated in the field. At this stage a powerful *dyschronicity* seems to dominate the relationship and each partner acts out one of the opposite polarities in the field; conscious and unconscious are now in open conflict in each partner and in the relationship, without arriving at a possible "coexistence." Hence feelings of guilt and/or shame emerge, which are often reactions to the collapse of idealized images of self, of the other, and of the relationship.

If the analyst is able to contain and manage the tension of the conflict and "side" with both partners, by seeing the opposites as a quality of the relationship and the *coniunctio* underway, and not as characteristics specific to each partner, then *Three* begins to enter the field. This helps the partners to observe the relationship as a force field, a third party that they both tend to form unknowingly, but which ultimately dominates and conditions them. This enables a new apex of observation to be constellated, which places the relationship itself in the center, while each partner enters into a deeper and more complex relationship with both polarities present in the field, with the lights and shadows that characterize self and other.

Now a further transformation is possible. Each of the participants in the session is able to experience a new sense of unity with themselves and, contemporaneously, with the other and the relationship in general, which seems to come into its own, independently of the psychic life of the individual partners. Thus *Four* is manifest in the field: the sense of totality, of a *unio molteplice*, in which each partner feels contained, but is more conscious of entering or leaving.

Now, a new sense of *coniunctio* can enter the relationship. The opposites, conscious and unconscious, are no longer con-fused as they were in the undifferentiated stage *One*, nor even split in the form of a dyad, as in stage *Two*. Instead, they coexist in a more fluid and harmonious system that has the structure of number *Four*. This is the experience of the *symbol*, which, as Trevi reminds us, does not operate a definitive synthesis between the opposites, between the time of the unconscious and of consciousness, but is rather a *systemic operation* capable of maintaining the tension between them without reducing one to the other (Trevi 1986). In this phase, the couple is able to form symbols that emerge in the dreams and fantasies of the partners – as exemplified by the couple who recounted a dream in which there appeared the image of a toy activated by two remote controls, one white and the other black. At this stage, which is never definitive for the life of the couple, *achronicity* and *chronicity* coexist and *synchronicity* and *dyschronicity* alternate more smoothly. We are now at the center of Stein's second schema (Stein, Chapter 3, p. 40) where the formation of the symbol and of an Ego-Self axis in the couple allows the partners to keep the opposites together in a more dialectic and fecund relationship (De Benedittis et al. 2019).

This phase is never conclusive, however, and the *coniunctio* cycle always repeats itself from one to four throughout the relationship, and even during a single session. We might say that it is precisely through the cyclicity of the *coniunctio* that the four temporality modalities come into being and that the symbol, cyclically formed by the partners, generates the maturative transformations of the couple.

Caramazza draws inspiration from Panikkar's thought to remind us that when "intensely experienced" the present always has a "transhistorical dimension" and can be considered "the temporal dimension of eternity" (Caramazza, Chapter 2, p. 17). Panikkar sees this as characterizing all of our "ecstatic experiences in the face of the mysteries of life, suffering, and death" (quoted by Caramazza, Chapter 2, p. 18), which certainly include the experience of love.

Note

All Elena Caramazza's writings have been translated in English by Susan Ann White.

Bibliography

Ballerini, A., Rossi Monti, M. (1990) *La vergogna e il delirio*, Bollati Boringhieri, Turin.

De Benedittis, F., Fersurella S., Presciuttini, S. (2019) *Orizzonti di coppia. Individuarsi con il partner. Un percorso analitico junghiano*, Moretti & Vitali, Bergamo.

Dicks, H.V. (1967) *Tensioni coniugali*, Borla, Roma (1992).

Jung, C.G. (1917/43) Psicologia dell'inconscio, in *Opere*, vol. VII, Bollati Boringhieri, Torino (1983).

Jung, C.G. (1925) Il matrimonio come relazione psicologica, in *Opere*, vol. XVII, Bollati Boringhieri, Torino (1991).

Kohut, H. (1971) *Narcisismo e analisi del Sé*, Bollati Boringhieri, Torino (2006).

Munari, F., La Scala, M. (1995) Significato e funzioni della vergogna, *Rivista di Psicoanalisi*, 41/1, 5–27.
Munari, F., La Scala, M. (2003) La honte. Voir l'autre me voir, *Revue Française de Psychanalyse*, 67, 1817–1822.
Schwartz-Salant, N. (1998) *La Relazione. Psicologia, clinica e terapia dei campi interattivi*, Vivarium, Milan (2002).
Trevi, M. (1986) *Metafore del simbolo*, Raffaello Cortina, Milan.
Von Franz, M.L. (1978) *L'esperienza del tempo*, Red Edizioni, Como (1996).

Pauli's 'The Piano Session' – A reading with musical accompaniment

Murray Stein

Scene 1

PAULI: It was a misty day, and I had been seriously troubled for some time. There were *two* schools: in the one they understood words but not meaning, and in the other they understood meaning but not *my* words. I couldn't bring the two schools, science and psyche, together. My last hope was to visit a young woman who lives in Kusnacht.

*

Scene 2

PAULI: When I arrived at her place and opened the door, I heard from afar a strong masculine voice. I knew it well. It was the voice of the Master. It always sounded to me like the voice of a ship's captain.

VOICE OF THE MASTER: *Time Reversal!*

PAULI: Immediately, I saw images that looked like cones pointing downwards and their openings facing upward. I recognized this from physics. This gave me confidence, so I went into the house.

*

Scene 3

PAULI: Suddenly I was back *in Vienna*! I was a schoolboy, and I was carrying a briefcase filled with sheets of music. Forty years had simply melted away. It was the year 1913.

I entered a room that contained a grand piano and other pieces of furniture as in the old days.

A lady with dark hair was standing by the piano. She looked like a trusted old friend. She was a distinguished lady, and I felt I should address her with great respect. When I approached her, she held out her hand and spoke to me.

LADY: You haven't been playing the piano for a long time. Let me give you a lesson.

PAULI: Yes, please do. Music would be good for me right now because I'm feeling troubled.

THE VOICE OF THE MASTER: (from the far distance) *Captain*!

LADY: (flustered at first, then calming down) Once upon a time there was a Captain ...

PAULI: Here in Vienna there is a Captain, and his daughter is ill, her soul is sick.

Now I see the Master approaching the Captain's house. He seems to be expecting the Captain to speak the words.

LADY: The words? Which words?

PAULI: *The* words! "Lord, I am not worthy to receive you in my house, but speak just one word and my servant will be healed."

There was once another Captain, in the town of Kapernaum, and he spoke these words.

LADY: What used to be the obvious thing to do in those times is not the same today. Those were ancient biblical times.

PAULI: Kapernaum or Vienna – it makes no difference. The problem is the same. The point is: the Captain in Vienna did *not* speak the necessary words. It was a simple matter. All he needed to do is say "my daughter" instead of "my servant." She would have been healed! But the Captain in Vienna belongs to a school in which words are understood but not meaning, so he could not find the right words to say when the Master wanted to come to him. So the Master turned away and left. It was a missed opportunity.

I think it must be very hard for the Master to make himself known to us, and even more difficult to make himself *understood* by us. We are strangers to him, as he is to us. To us, it looks like he's dreaming, like a sleepwalker who is perfectly sure of himself. I believe he doesn't know much about our waking lives, but he has a vague notion and he wants to know more. He wants his world and ours to come closer together, and this is what he is constantly trying to arrange. He doesn't mind turning away once in a while, but this time it's serious. This is enough to really harm the Captain in Vienna and his daughter.

LADY: (cutting in): Yes, but now he's trying something else. He just told me I should help you to play the piano better. This will ease the situation. I also caught his words, "beyond the censorship," but I didn't understand what he means.

PAULI: (interrupting) Oh, I understand that. Do you remember *Freud?*

LADY: Yes, of course. He was my counselor – but he didn't know it.

PAULI: You see, Freud believed there was a censor that is always present but only shows itself in dreams. He also thought it was the product of a moralistic Victorian aunt who is otherwise invisible. But actually such a moralistic aunt doesn't exist. But censorship in dreams does exist. (In a low voice) It's created by professors, particularly by those in the sciences. This is because the old Captain of Kopenick doesn't have power anymore – thank God! However, there is one exception.

LADY: What do you mean? Who was the Captain of Kopenick?

PAULI: The Captain of Kopenick was the archetypal charlatan. Nowadays it is the name for the whole group of charlatans into whose traps so many people have fallen. They are numerous in heaven and on earth. When I was in primary school, I believed there was only one charlatan, the Captain of Kopenick, but later I learned that there are many. But this phoney Captain is possible only because there are true Captains and true Masters. He is a fake copy! There are false and true Captains and Masters in the world.

LADY: You spoke about an exception. What did you mean? The charlatan Captain has lost his power, but is there another one?

PAULI: (without hesitation) Yes, exactly. Today you find a new Captain of Kopenick in the East, in a sect of virulent ideologues.

They are the red slaves. They are dangerous because they have guns and canons. The black robed Jesuits have to make do without that kind of power today, and they also have to do without the stake. Let me explain: This is important for understanding dream censorship.

It goes like this: The Master sends me dreams of scientific meetings in Russia that take place under police surveillance, where the police prevent most participants from talking.

Of course, the Master wants to tell me about myself, not about the red slaves in Russia. It is a metaphor. In particular he wants me to understand how the rigidly held but quite limited current views in my mind (the "theories") enforce censorship internally.

Since the Captain in Vienna, who is in charge of the science teachers, did not speak the words and the Master turned away, the Master now wants to assert himself again, and he seems to find *me* particularly suited for this purpose. Through me, he wants to come out into the light of day at all costs! I must say, I often feel weird, and I'm frightened of him. He's not only good; he can also be dangerous. And he's most dangerous when you ignore him, as the Captain in Vienna did. So, on the one hand, I'm afraid of the Master; on the other hand, he fascinates me. I can't keep away from him, as he can't stay away from me.

LADY: My attitude towards him is quite different. We are as one.

PAULI: For a long time I believed that was the right way, but I changed my mind.

There was a charlatan Captain who told people that the black keys on the piano are just holes where white keys are missing, and that all the so-called Masters are either completely white or completely black. Many people still follow this line of dogmatic thinking, but not me. I don't agree.

LADY: (laughs loudly) You should tell them that we can also play minor chords on the white keys – such as A C E – and major chords on the black keys – such as F-sharp A-sharp C-sharp. The truth is more complex than they want to know. Both black and white keys have their reality.

All that really matters is that you know how to play the piano.

PAULI: (speaks to the audience) I played faithfully and willingly as she had taught me. And when I looked at her, I noticed that she had Oriental eyes. She reminded me of the Chinese woman of my dreams.

Now that I realize more fully that the art of playing the piano is all that matters, the censorship has eased off considerably. I can relax. The Master immediately sent me images showing the Russian armies being pushed back after heavy fighting. Later I even got images in which the Russians retreated voluntarily. My theories are losing their dogmatic grip! The Iron Curtain in me is no longer so impenetrable.

There are small and large gaps in it, peepholes through which I can look. Through one of these I saw the Captain in Kapernaum and in Vienna and the Master approaching them.

LADY: Now I see a vast landscape.

It used to be under water, but now the water has receded, and while the land is still somewhat wet the ground is firm. It stretches to the far north. Strange people inhabit it. It is becoming more visible.

PAULI: I see it too, and I see the Master there. He is distributing papers among the people. I can't read them, but they can. These papers probably tell them their names and who they are. They are becoming more aware of their specific identities.

LADY: Now I feel that the black keys want to contribute major chords. Please play F- sharp A-sharp C-sharp.

PAULI: (slowly) I have the impression that the white keys are like the words and the black keys are the meaning: science and soul. At times the words of science are sad and the meaning of soul is joyful, then at other times it is just the other way around. But somehow they are coordinated. Here, with you, it's not like it is in the place where there are two schools that give me so much trouble. Here I see that there is only *one* piano, with white keys and black keys. Words and meaning come together on this piano.

LADY: (in a soft voice) I have to confess that I can only play the piano. I understand nothing of *your* numbers, the language of the science school. But they say that numbers are like tones. I can understand what you told me about the censorship. The Censors want to understand the world without meaning. They want to exclude the soul. But it's evident that one must play differently according to how warm it is and what is constellated by the Master. According to how one plays, it will be more or less warm. For example, a while ago it got quite hot when the Master said "Captain." Meaning emerges when it gets warm. How can you understand the world without including meaning? It's absurd.

PAULI: The Censors nowadays believe that *chance* rules the world; I mean the best of the Censors.

LADY: But do they believe that chance is always the same? Doesn't it change when it gets warm?

PAULI: (thoughtfully) Chance is always fluctuating, but sometimes it does so systematically. I guess this is what you mean. Sometimes chance fluctuates with meaning and purpose.

*

PAULI: With these words a big change comes about.

Through the window I see people approaching the house. They line up near the window and call my name. At first their faces are unfamiliar; I do not recognize any of them. I play an easy piece by Bach to keep everything orderly.

*

PAULI: I realize I have no choice. I *have* to give a lecture. I open the window. Now I am no longer in Vienna but in Zurich, and it is 1953. I speak from the window and give what I call

A LECTURE TO STRANGERS

It seems to me that attempts to extend the viewpoints of modern science will lead to a new type of natural law. I have in mind the meaningful coincidences brought to our attention by C. G. Jung, which cannot be reproduced intentionally and only occur in special circumstances. With these the element of meaning is introduced into random chance events. Naturally this affects developments in evolution. The mutations are not only random, but they show a pattern of meaningful coincidences. By naming these coincidences "synchronistic," Jung acknowledges a peculiar relation between them and our *notion of time*. They take place in the world of time and space. To the extent that the phenomena of adaptation in biological evolution clearly demonstrate a direction in time, it seems quite natural to consider them as connected with meaning, or purpose.

In spite of the lively demands from the audience that I go on and speak further, I close the window. Now I am alone again with the lady.

LADY: (with astonishment and urgency) That was very moving. I think we have just created something! Now it must be made *legitimate*! This new creation needs a name, an identity.

PAULI: When one really wants to introduce something new like this to the world, one has to offer something concrete so people can experience and verify it for themselves directly. They need to put their hands on it and test its reality. All I can tell them at this point, unfortunately, is that chance sometimes changes in a systematic way, but I can't yet explain to them the psychic reality that you speak of when you use the words, "it's getting warm."

I can't explain how one can study this phenomenon scientifically. Without that, this would look more like a *magical* procedure than the basis for scientific experiment. To begin with, I will have to explain to them in a way that they can understand in their school what is meant by the "piano" and "piano playing." No doubt they will have a different understanding of this and hear different tones than we do. I have to work out a comprehensible language for them.

LADY: I have to confess that I am limited. I can only play the piano and teach it. I can neither teach piano theory nor can I construct one. This is beyond my capacities.

PAULI: Let's start like this: The human being is like this piano in front of us.

The *tones* have pitch and intensity. The *melodies* are patterns that can be reproduced and recognized in different keys because one key can be transformed into another. This makes the language of emotion and meaning communicable.

Second, just as there are *low, medium, and high tones* on the piano, you find in human beings the *instinctive* or impulsive, the *intellectual* or rational, and the *spiritual* or supernatural tonalities. We have these *three levels of tonality*.

To continue, the *volume of sound* is the intensity with which these tones act upon consciousness. They can be *low, medium, or loud*, and they can vary from time to time.

I know of a school that instead of melodies or tones speaks of *typical primordial images* (archetypes) – these are the patterns as they manifest in the psyche. Moreover, instead of tonal pitches it speaks of colors, which are *emotions*. And instead of soft or loud sounds, it speaks of light and heavy psychic *masses* (complexes).

The common feature of all these images and melodies is *number*.

Earlier you said you understand nothing of *our* numbers. Do you know of *other* numbers?

LADY: (thoughtful): I am not sure, but I guess so. For me, numbers and tones are really one and the same. If the *pitch* of a tone were one number, and the *volume* of sound were another, then I could actually count them, and the *melody* would result in a pattern of numbers. But it's seldom that I can transpose my impressions exactly into numbers and communicate them to you.

PAULI: And I cannot play the piano like you. As you can see, I can only play simple pieces, not complicated sonatas. And you don't know mathematics.

If I had more of your skill and you more of mine, you would be able to communicate number patterns to me and I would be able to do calculations with them. These archetypal patterns reach down into the world of animals and plants, perhaps even deeper.

They might indicate precisely "how warm it is" – to use your words – the emergence of meaning. Feeling one's way into their varying configurations would show lines of emerging development.

They would have to leave space for different possible lines of development and would in general only indicate a disposition or probability for what might result, not a certainty. This would not lead to a new type of determinism. One would always have to assume a certain amount of freedom for what could happen, in particular with respect to the choice of the "key" in which a "melody" is realized.

But if we could develop the ability to perceive these configurations and to understand them, we would see more clearly how the fluctuations of chance come and go in nature in such a way that they allow meaning or purpose to become manifest.

Then, I'm sure, the Captain would speak the right word at the right moment, and so would the Master. And the Captain's daughter would be healed!

LADY: And the young woman you told me about would be free to live.

PAULI: *Yes.* And then we would also know more about that country in the far North, which we can see only in outline now, and would also know more about its inhabitants.

But today I have seen that home country from afar. Doesn't the home country belong inseparably to the Master? And just like the Master changes his form over time – from past to present to future – so there is a past and a present and a future home country, just like there is a past, a present and a future face of woman. These images change over time. (pause).

Now I'm sad, because like so many others I see the home country from afar, but I will not enter it.

LADY: But that's ok.

You forget something very important, namely the fourth, the timeless. It belongs to the home country and to the feminine. This creates unity among the three parts you were just talking about.

PAULI: Your words stir me profoundly.

Sadly, though, I have to get back to my world now. But I will return.

LADY: What do you want to do there?

PAULI: I want to try with all the means available to me to bring about a state of reconciliation with the Master, so the two schools can be united.

VOICE OF THE MASTER: That is what I have *long* been waiting for.

PAULI: Then, when he is reconciled to our world you will be free!

LADY: (astonished): What do you mean? Are you alluding to what I said earlier about being one with the Master?

PAULI: Exactly. You will have freedom to move about and make your own choices.

Goodbye, for now. To whatever extent I am able to confront the world in the future, I owe it all to you. I now feel it is time to leave.

VOICE OF THE MASTER: Wait! Transformation of the center!

PAULI: (with astonishment) In earlier times one would have announced, "behold, lead is transformed into gold!"

At this moment, the Lady slips a ring from her finger, which I had not noticed before, and lets it float in the air.

LADY: I suppose you know this ring from your school of mathematics. It is the *Ring i.*

PAULI: Yes, of course. The *i* creates a united pair of the *Void* and the *One*, the *imaginary* and the *real* numbers.

LADY: It makes the *instinctive*, the *intellectual*, and the *spiritual* into something whole. Real numbers and imaginary numbers alone cannot represent this wholeness without the *i*.

PAULI: The ring with the *i* is the unity beyond particle and wave, and at the same time it is the operation that brings one of these two forms into the foreground.

LADY: It is the atom, the inDivisible unit of wholeness.

PAULI: It makes time stop, turns time into a static image.

LADY: It is the marriage of the imaginary and the real, and it is the realm of the middle that one can never reach alone but only in a pair.

VOICE OF THE MASTER: Gracious Lady, *remain merciful!*

PAULI: Now I knew that I could leave the room and go back into normal time and everyday life.

*

Scene 4

PAULI: Now I am outside, and I notice I am wearing my coat and hat. Suddenly, from afar, I hear a C-major chord of four notes – apparently it is being played by the Lady who is now alone again.

The End

Index

Abraham, model of man of faith 62
"acausal correspondences" 22
acceptance 49; of reality 62–3;
  self-acceptance 42–3
achronicity xii, xiii, 71–2; achronistic
  time xiv; in love relationship 76,
  77, 81, 83; myth and 22–3;
  temporality and 20, 21, 22–5,
  27, 29, 30, 32, 37, 38, 41
active imagination 5–8; experience of 61
Acts 2:4 42
Adam and Eve xiii, xv; temporality
  and 23–4, 25–6, 29, 41
Adler, G. 22, 23
adulthood, synchronicity and
  establishment of 74
affective sphere, atrophy of 49–50
Aion (Jung, C.G.) 66
Aite, P. 51
Alice's Adventures in Wonderland
  (Carroll, L.) 19
Allen, W. 33
Analytical Psychology Treatise
  (Carotenuto, A., Ed.) 55
Answer to Job (Jung, C.G.) 59,
  61, 63
Antichrist of Christian theology 60
archetypes 41, 60–61, 65, 72, 87, 91
Atmanspacher. H. 22
Atmanspacher, H. and Fach, W. 3, 12
Atmanspacher, H., Primas, H. and
  Wertenschlag-Birkhäuser, E. 11
Atropos 16, 17–18
autoneplophilia ('adult baby
  syndrome') 33–4

Balint, M. 31
Ballerini, A. and Rossi Monti, M.
  79, 80
Beethoven, L. van 1
"In the beginning" (Genesis 1:1) 23
Being, fullness of xv
Benedict, R. 27
bereavement, time and 17–18
beta elements 31
betrayal, effects of 77–8, 79–80
The Bible and biblical narrative xiii,
  23–4, 41–2
Bion, W. 31
black keys xi; language of meaning,
  black keys representative of 7;
  musical accompaniment, a reading
  with 88–9
Blumenberg, H. 23, 72
Brihadaranyaka Upanishad 68–9
Buber, M. 63

Cain and Abel 26
Cambray, J. 12, 22
Candide (Voltaire) 64
Captain of Kopenick (archetypal
  charlatan) 87
Caramazza, E. xi, xii, xiii, xiv,
  xv, xvi–xvii, 57; afterword,
  mentions in 71, 73, 76, 77, 78, 83;
  correspondence between Stein and
  54–5; evil, reflections on problem
  of 65–70; premise xvi–xvii;
  synchronicity as bridge between
  achronicity and chronicity 46–55;
  time dimensions, comparison

between Panikkar and Jung on 15–18
cat and kittens, synchronistic match-ups between 47–8
causality: causal links between past and present 26; sycnhronicity and, uniting of 7–8; synchronicity and, inextricably interwoven dimensions of 15; synchronicity and, interplay of 1; synchronicity and, relationship between 3–4
censorship 87, 88, 89
Cervantes, M. de 33
chance: chance events, meaning and 4; musical accompaniment, a reading with 89
childhood memory, re-emergence of 47–8
Christianity, cultural effects of 63
chronicity xiii, xv, 72; advantages for humankind in 29; chronistic temporality, entry into 51–2; inner and outer, overlapping of 31; in love relationship 77, 78, 79, 83; temporality and 20, 21, 23, 24, 25–9, 30, 32, 34, 35–6, 37, 38, 40, 42, 43
chronological memory 38
chronological time 71; life and moving between achronistic mode and 25
The Chrysanthemum and the Sword (Benedict, R.) 27
clinical experience, synchronicity interrupted in 51–2
collective power of evil 60
collective unconscious, psyche and Self at level of 53
complexes 35, 36, 60–61, 91; activated complex, past and present events in 35; autonomous complexes in psyche 34; shame, complex of 31
confession 77, 89, 90
conflict definition 81–2
conjunction (coniunctio): in couple therapy 80–83; progression of 81; repetitiveness of 83; synchronicity and 73–4
Connolly, A. 12, 22, 31

consciousness 71, 72; chronicity and 26–7; conscious life, discontinuity between unconscious psychic time and 34–5; discriminatory capacity of 72; Ego as center of 52; fostering a symbolic attitude to 16; life and 68; lowering level of 75; the unconscious and 4
Corbin, H. 22
couple relationship 74–6
courtship, early stages of 75
Creation, God and 67
"creation in time," acts of 2, 4
creation myths 22
creativity: causality and 15–16; creative (or mystic) states 72
Crime and Punishment (Dostoyevsky, F.M.) 27
Curatorium of C.G. Jung Institute 56

De Benedittis, F., Fersurella S. and Presciuttini, S. 71–84
dementia 24, 29, 72
depth psychology 43, 53; ethics and 57; evil-doing and 57–8; quantum physics and 1, 3, 8
Depth Psychology and a New Ethic (Neumann, E.) 58, 60, 61–2, 63
determinism 29, 91
Deus absconditus of nature 68
Dicks, H.V. 75
Divine Wisdom 54
Divinity, achronistic temporality and 23
Don Quixote (Cervantes, M. de) 33
Dostoyevsky, F.M. 27
Duras, M. xiv–xv
Dusinberre, E. 1
dyschronicity xiii, xiv–xv, 72–3; cases of 34–7; in love relationship 76, 77–8, 82, 83; temporal experience in 73; temporality and 20, 22, 29, 32–4, 35–6, 38, 43n1

Edelman, S.P. 27, 30
Ego: anima and, union of 9; development of 27–8; evil-doing and 57–8
Ego and Self, guilt, shame and dialogue between 53

Ego-consciousness: modalities of temporality, awareness of 38; self-assertion and 59–60; unconscious and, connection between 5–6; union of unconscious with 9–10

Ego-Self axis 74; effect on shame 41, 42, 43

Ego-transcendence 43

Einstein, A. 2

Eliade, M. 22, 23

emotions 16, 48, 49, 50, 68, 74–5, 91; emotional attachment 75; emotional life (and reactions) 35

empathy deficiency 48–51

"episodic memory": "semantic consciousness" and 28; temporality and 25–6

epistolary dialogues xi

eternity: present as temporal dimension of 17; time dimensions, comparison between Panikkar and Jung on 15

ethics 29; of individuation 63; problem of evil and issue of 56–7, 61, 63

Europe (Germany and Soviet Union), problem of evil and 59

European Enlightenment 2

events, dating of 72

evil: cerebral "centers" of 53–4; ethics and, Jung's preoccupation with 63; God's Shadow in 67–8; unfathomable mystery of xvii

evil, Jung and Neumann on "problem" of 56–64; Abraham, model of man of faith 62; active imagination, experience of 61; *Answer to Job* (Jung, C.G.) 59, 61, 63; Antichrist of Christian theology 60; *Candide* (Voltaire) 64; Christianity, cultural effects of 63; collective power of evil 60; depth psychology, ethics and 57; depth psychology, evil-doing and 57–8; *Depth Psychology and a New Ethic* (Neumann, E.) 58, 60, 61–2, 63; Ego, evil-doing and 57–8; Ego-consciousness, self-assertion and 59–60; ethics, issue of 56; Europe (Germany and

Soviet Union), problem of evil and 59; evil and ethics, Jung's preoccupation with 63; evil-other, perceptions of 58; faith, mystical moment of encounter and realization in leap of 62–3; Godhead 61, 62, 63, 64; Godhead, advocacy for integration of evil into 63–4; human consciousness, Neumann and overestimation of capacities of 60; identification with good, unconsciousness of shadow of evil within 58; innocent evil-doing 57; Jewish people, period of maximum threat to 59, 61–2; *Lunar Conscience* (Stein, M.) 57; Mephisto 60; *New Ethic,* agreement (almost) on 60; new morality, advocacy for 58–9; opposites, problem of 59–60, 61; "problem of evil," indelible inscription in human concern 56; psychology, problem of evil for 56; Satan 60, 63; unconsciousness, root of all evil 58; Yahweh, myth of 61

evil, reflections on problem of: *Aion* (Jung, C.G.) 66; Brihadaranyaka Upanishad 68–9; consciousness, life and 68; Creation, God and 67; Deus absconditus of nature 68; evil, God's Shadow in 67–8; existence, reality of 67; God, justice and 66; God, Self and 65; guilt, evil and atonement for 65–6; guilt, Judeo-Christian tradition and origin of 69; Job, God-image for 67–8; Judeo-Christian tradition 66; metaphysical and psychological aspects of evil, inseparability of 65; myths of Yahweh and Prajapati, comparison of 68–9; Panikkar's reflections 66, 69; Prajapati, Indian myth of 68–9; Prajapati, myth of 68–9; psyche, "collective man" and 66; reciprocal belonging, relationship of God and man 69; redemption, evil and 65–6, 69; Shiva 66; Yahweh, myth of 66, 67, 68–9

evil-other, perceptions of 58

existence, reality of 67

faith, mystical moment of 62–3
Faulkner, W. 33
Faust (Goethe, J.W.) 10, 18
Fersurella, S. 71–84
Fitzmyer, J. 42
freedom 91–2; from laws of nature 8
Freud, S. 87
fusional couples, dynamics of 75–6

Galatians 2:20 42
Garden of Eden xiii; temporality and 24, 25, 29, 41
Genesis, biblical Book of 23, 41
God: justice and 66; Self and 65
Goddess Reason, enshrinement of 2
Godhead 61, 62; advocacy for integration of evil into 63–4
Goethe, J.W. 10, 18, 60
Greek Moirai 16
Green, A. 31
guilt: atonement for evil and 65–6; couple relationship and 77–80; Ego development and 27–8; Judeo-Christian tradition and origin of 69; persecutory feelings of 79; Shadow and 76; shame and, separation of 79

Hinton, L. 19, 24, 25, 31, 36, 37, 43n3, 78
Hiroshima mon amour (Duras, M.) xiv–xv
historical inertia, destiny and 16
human consciousness: Neumann and overestimation of capacities of 60; time dimensions and 15–16

I Ching 4
"iconic constancy" 72; myth as 23
imago Dei 42
in illo tempore ('in that time') 22, 23, 24
individuation 19, 28, 36, 37, 74, 76; ethics of 63; temporality and 42–3; transcendent function and 38, 42–3
infancy, syntony between inner and outer worlds of 30; *see also* mother-infant relationship
injustice xiv, 67

inner harmonies, blockage of xi
inner world, reconstruction of positivity within 50–51
innocent evil-doing 57
instinctive tonalities 91, 93
intellect, discriminating faculty of 15
intellectual tonalities 91, 93
Iron Curtain 88
Izutsu, T. 42

Japan, separation of Ego from unconscious in 27
Jehle-Wildberger, M. 63
Jesus Christ 41–2
Jewish people, period of maximum threat to 59, 61–2
Job, God-image for 67–8
Judeo-Christian tradition: evil, reflections on problem of 66; myth of 54
Jung, C.G.: afterword, mentions in 74, 75, 76, 80–81; evil, reflections on problem of 65–7, 68; music for another age, Pauli's "Piano Lesson" 2, 3, 4, 9; "problem of evil," Neumann and Jung on 56, 58–9, 60–64; rhizome, life and 18; synchronicity as bridge between achronicity and chronicity 52, 55; temporality, modalities of, problem of shame and 22, 23, 28, 30, 31, 32–3, 37, 38, 41, 42; time dimensions, comparison with Panikkar on 15, 16, 18; wartime experience, temporality and 32–3
Jung, C.G. and Jaffe, A. 32–3
Jung, C.G. and Neumann, E. 59, 60, 61, 62, 64
Jung, C.G. and Pauli, W. 12

Kafka, F. 27
kairòs 15; *kronos* and 17, 18, 31
Kapernaum, Captain in 88–9
Kaufman, G. 30
Kawai, H. 27
Keller, A. 63
Kierkegaard, S. 62
Klitsner, Y.S. 12
Kohut, H. 79
Kronos-Saturn 21

Laboratorio Analitico per Immagini 51
landscape with strange people 88–9
language of meaning, black keys
  representative of 7
Laplanche, J. and Pontalis, J.-B. 28
lecture to the strangers (Pauli)
  8–9, 90
Levi-Strauss, C. 27
love relationship: achronicity in 76,
  77, 81, 83; betrayal, effects of
  77–8, 79–80; chronicity in 77, 78,
  79, 83; conflict definition 81–2;
  conjunction *(coniunctio)*, progression of 81; conjunction
  (coniunctio), repetitiveness of 83;
  conjunction *(coniunctio)* in couple
  therapy 80–83; consciousness, lowering level of 75; couple relationship 74–6; courtship, early stages
  of 75; dyadic membrane in couples
  75; dyschronicity in 76, 77–8, 82,
  83; fusional couples, dynamics of
  75–6; guilt, couple relationship
  77–80; guilt, persecutory feelings
  of 79; guilt, Shadow and 76; guilt,
  shame and, separation of 79; marriage, psychological relationship in
  75; meaningful coincidences 75;
  mother, syntony with 78–9; past-
  present-future continuum 78; psychic dynamics of falling in love 75;
  relationship quality, conjunction
  (coniunctio) and 82; reparative
  guilt feelings 79; self-esteem, modulation of 78; Shadow, dark side in
  76; shame, anger and 80; shame,
  couple relationship 77–80; shame,
  guilt feelings and, separation of 79;
  shame, Shadow and 76; shame,
  unworthiness and 78; symbols,
  systemic operation and experience
  of 82–3; synchronicity in 81, 83;
  synchronistic events, occurrence of
  79–80; temporality, modalities in
  couples 74–6; temporality and
  symbol formation in couple
  therapy 80–83
Luke 23:34 57
Lunar Conscience (Stein, M.) 57
lysis of the story 11

Macrobius 21
magical procedure 90
Magid, S. 42
Main, R. 22
marriage, psychological relationship
  in 75
Master: Masters, Captains and 87;
  reassertion of, need for 87–8; voice
  of 85, 86, 87, 88–9, 92, 93
maternal mental absence, nightmare
  and shame of 51–2
Mazdean (Zoroastrian) book of
  Genesis 22
meaning: but not words, school of
  understanding of 85; discovery of
  xi–xii; meaningful coincidences 2,
  75; and synchronicity, problem of
  3; words and xvi
Meier, C.A. 3, 4
melodies 91
Memories, Dreams, Reflections (Jung,
  C.G.) 32, 37
memory 21, 24, 26, 33, 35, 36, 49, 50,
  54–5, 71–2, 78; absence of 41;
  childhood memory 28, 47; chronological memory 38; collective
  memory 56; continuity of 20, 25,
  28, 46, 47–8; episodic memory 25,
  28; narrative of 31; repressed
  memory 21
Mephisto 60
Mercurius 9, 38
mercy 93
Midnight in Paris (Woody Allen
  film) 33
Milkmaid (Vermeer painting) xii
mind-matter correlations, structural-
  phenomenological typology of 12
mnemonic capacities 71, 72
modernity, synchronicity theory and
  2, 4
Montale, E. xiii–xiv
mother, syntony with 78–9
mother and infant: relationship
  between xiii, 73; synchronistic
  match-ups between 31, 46–7
Munari, F. and La Scala, M. 79
music for a future age 12
"Music for a Later Age" (Stein, M.)
  1–14

musical accompaniment, a reading with: archetypes 91; black keys 88–9; Captain of Kopenick (archetypal charlatan) 87; censorship 87, 88, 89; chance 89; complexes 91; confession 89, 90; determinism 91; emotions 91; freedom 91–2; Freud, Sigmund 87; instinctive tonalities 91, 93; intellectual tonalities 91, 93; Iron Curtain 88; Kapernaum, Captain in 88–9; Lady, voice of 86–93; landscape with strange people 88–9; legitimacy 90; magical procedure 90; Master, reassertion of, need for 87–8; Master, voice of the 85, 86, 87, 88–9, 92, 93; meaning but not words, school of understanding of 85; melodies 91; mercy 93; numbers, imaginary 93; numbers, number patterns and 91; numbers, real 93; Pauli, voice of 85–93; pitch 91; probability 91; reconciliation 92; the "ring *i*" 93; Russia and Russians 87, 88; sound, volume of 91; spiritual tonalities 91, 93; time, notion of 90; time reversal 85; tonality, levels of 91; transformation 92–3; understanding 86, 87, 90; Vienna, Captain in 66, 86, 87; white keys 88–9; wholeness 93; words 85, 86–7, 89, 90, 91, 92; words but not meaning, school of understanding of 85

musical chords, image of xi

Mysterium Coniunctionis (Jung, C.G.) 43n5

mystical conjunction 37

myths: achronistic temporality 23; of Yahweh and Prajapati, comparison of 68–9

nature, laws of 3

Neumann, E. 5–7, 11, 55, 65; "problem of evil," Jung and Neumann on 56, 58, 59, 61, 62, 63, 64; reality, Neumann's planes (or stages) of 5; temporality, modalities of, problem of shame and 30, 40; *unus mundus,* awareness of 6

neuroscience, "episodic memory" and 25–6

New Ethic, agreement (almost) on 60

new morality, advocacy for 58–9

New Testament 41–2

Newtonian modern physics 74

noontide moments xv

nostalgia, dyschronicity and 33

numbers 9–10, 26, 38, 89, 91, 93

objective meaning, notion of 2

Oedipus, myth of 16–17

Ōhrmazd 22

opposites, problem of 59–60, 61

Panikkar, R. xi, xiii, xvi–xvii, 15–16, 17–18, 83; evil, reflections on problem of 66, 69

parental recognition, sense of existence and 49

past-present-future continuum 78

St. Paul 42

Pauli, W. xi; active imagination, change in 8; afterword, mentions in 74, 80–81; causality, absolute rule of 8; chance, blindness of 8; creativity, purpose of 8–9; Ego and anima, union of 9; lecture to the strangers 8–9, 90; music for another age, "The Piano Lesson" 1, 2, 3, 4, 5–8, 9–10, 11, 12, 13; musical accompaniment, a reading with 85–93; mutations, anomaly in pattern of 8–9; mysticism and science, embodiment in 2; quantum physics 8; temporality, modalities of, problem of shame and 22, 38, 40–41, 43; voice of 85–93

Pavoni, C. xi–xv, 18

'The Piano Lesson' (Pauli, W.) xi, xvi, 1, 3, 4, 74; as active imagination 5–8; causality and sycnhronicity, uniting of 7–8; characters in 6–7; composition of 3; Ego-consciousness and the unconscious, connection between 5–6; Ego-consciousness (the unit), union of unconscious (the void) with 9–10; ending of, open question concerning 11–12; inner and

outer levels, synchronicity and causality in 12; language of meaning, black keys representative of 7; lysis of the story 11; music for a future age 12; personality, centering on 7; positivistic science, white keys representative of 7; real numbers, imaginary numbers and 9–10; the "ring i" 9–11, 38–9; structural-phenomenological typology of mind-matter correlations 12; time reversal in beginning of 6; white keys as words, black keys as meaning 6
pitch 91
Platonic year 40–41
positivistic science: synchronicity, problem of 2; white keys representative of 7; see also quantum physics
Prajapati, Indian myth of xv, 68–9
Presciuttini, S. 71–84
probability 8, 29, 91
psyche: "collective man" and 66; eternal time of xi; love, psychic dynamics of falling in 75; matter and, synchronicity and 3; subjective responsibility for destiny and 16
"The Psyche and the Transformation of the Reality Planes" (Newmann, E.) 5–6
psychoanalysis xvi, 2, 43n1, 79
psychology: achronicity, psychological temporality 21; problem of evil for 56
Psychology and Alchemy (Jung, C.G.) 2

quantum physics xvi; depth psychology and 1, 3; synchronicity, problem of 2

real numbers, imaginary numbers and 9–10
reality: acceptance of 62–3; discontinuous nature of 16; "reality principle," Ego and 28–9
reciprocal belonging, relationship of God and man 69
reconciliation 33, 78, 92

redemption, evil and 65–6, 69
reflections, harmony of xii
regression therapy, exploration of 36
relationship quality, conjunction and 82
La Relazione (Schwartz-Salant, N.) 81
religion, release from modalities of temporality and 42–3
reparation 35–6; reparative guilt feelings 79
retro-fantasizing (zurückphantasieren) 28
rhizome, life and 18
Ricoeur, P. 27
Rijksmuseum xii
the "ring i" 9–11, 38–9; musical accompaniment, a reading with 93
Roloff, L. 43n6
Romans 7:24–5 42
Rome xi; AIPA Center in xvi
Russia and Russians 87, 88

Satan 60, 63
Schellinski, K. 36
Schwartz-Salant, N. 81
science: mathematical time of xi; spirituality and, unification of 1
seasons, changing of 21
Self: chronistic temporality of 53–4; Jungian sense of 15
Self-Ego dialogue, assimilation of shame and 52–4
self-esteem, modulation of 78
"semantic consciousness" 28
Shadow, dark side in 76
shame: achronicity and 25; anger and 80; couple relationship and 77–80; early and preverbal experience of 30–31; guilt and, transformation of 36–7; guilt feelings and, separation of 79; in human experience 43; humility and 38; maternal mental absence, nightmare and shame of 51–2; Self-Ego dialogue and assimilation of 52–4; Shadow and 76; shame-cultures, guilt and 28; temporality and, psychological connection between 19; temporality and development of 35–6; unworthiness and 78

Shiva 66
Silenzio a Praga (Caramazza, E.)
54n1, 66–9
Singer, T. and Kaplinski, C. 36
sound, volume of 91
spiritual tonalities 91, 93
Stein, M. xi–xii, xiii, xiv, xv, xvi–xvii;
afterword, mentions in 75–6, 77,
78, 80–81, 82; correspondence
between Caramazza and 54–5;
music for another age, Pauli's
"Piano Lesson" 1–14; "problem of
evil," Neumann and Jung on
56–64; temporality, modalities of,
problem of shame and 19–45;
temporality, overview of modalities
of 71–4
Studi Junghiani journal 1
symbols, systemic operation and
experience of 82–3
"symphonicity" 1, 9
synchronicity xiii, 72–3; champagne
without bubbles, world without
12–13; extraordinary time and 74;
in love relationship 81, 83;
meaningful coincidence and 74;
phenomenon of xi–xii; preludes to
46–8; synchronistic events,
occurrence of 79–80; synchronistic
experience 1–2; temporal
experience in 73; temporality and
20, 22, 29–31, 32, 35, 37, 38
"Synchronicity: An Acausal Connecting Principle" (Jung, C.G.) 4
synchronicity, problem of 1–4; causality and synchronicity, relationship between 3–4; chance events,
meaning and 4; consciousness, the
unconscious and 4; "creation in
time," acts of 2; creation in time,
synchronicity as acts of 4; diagram
by Jung and Pauli 4; meaning and
synchronicity 3; "meaningful coincidences" 2; modernity, synchronicity theory and 2, 4; nature, laws
of 3; objective meaning, notion of
2; positivistic science 2; psyche and
matter, synchronicity and 3; quantum physics 2; synchronicitic
events 3; synchronistic experience

1–2; theoretical physics, revolution
in 2
synchronicity as bridge between
achronicity and chronicity 46–55;
affective sphere, atrophy of 49–50;
cat and kittens, synchronistic
match-ups between 47–8; childhood memory, re-emergence of
47–8; chronistic temporality, entry
into 51–2; clinical experience, synchronicity interrupted 51–2; collective unconscious, psyche and
Self at level of 53; consciousness,
Ego as center of 52; Divine
Wisdom 54; Ego and Self, guilt,
shame and dialogue between 53;
empathy deficiency 48–51; evil,
cerebral "centers" of 53–4; inner
world, reconstruction of positivity
within 50–51; Judeo-Christian
myth 54; maternal mental absence,
nightmare and shame of 51–2;
mother and infant, synchronistic
match-ups between 46–7; parental
recognition, sense of existence and
49; Self, chronistic temporality of
53–4; Self-Ego dialogue, assimilation of shame and 52–4; shame,
Self-Ego dialogue and assimilation
of 52–4; synchronicity, preludes to
46–8
"Synchronizing Time and Eternity"
(Stein, M.) 1
Szymborska, W. xii

"tempiternity" xi, xii–xiii, xvii–xviii;
time dimensions, comparison
between Panikkar and Jung on 15
temporal continuum, synchronicity
and 74
temporality, modalities of, problem
of shame and: "acausal correspondences" 22; acceptance 42;
achronicity 20, 21, 22–5, 27, 29,
30, 32, 37, 38, 41; achronicity,
myth and 22–3; activated complex,
past and present events in 35;
Adam and Eve 23–4, 25–6, 29, 41;
autoneplophilia ('adult baby syndrome') 33–4; "In the beginning"

(Genesis 1:1) 23; beta elements 31; The Bible and biblical narrative 23–4, 41–2; Cain and Abel 26; causal links between past and present 26; chronicities overlapping of inner and outer 31; chronicity 20, 21, 23, 24, 25–9, 30, 32, 34, 35–6, 37, 38, 40, 42, 43; chronicity, advantages for humankind in 29; chronological memory 38; chronological time, life and moving between achronistic mode and 25; *The Chrysanthemum and the Sword* (Benedict, R.) 27; conscious life, discontinuity between unconscious psychic time and 34–5; consciousness, chronicity and 26–7; creation myths 22; *Crime and Punishment* (Dostoyevsky, F.M.) 27; definitions 20–22; Divinity, achronistic temporality and 23; *Don Quixote* (Cervantes, M. de) 33; dyshronicity 20, 22, 29, 32–4, 35–6, 38, 43n1; dyshronicity, two cases of 34–7; Ego-consciousness aware of all four modalities 38; Ego development 27; Ego-Self axis, effect on shame 41, 42, 43; Ego-teanscendence 43; "episodic memory" 25–6; "episodic memory," "semantic consciousness" 28; Garden of Eden 24, 25, 29, 41; Genesis, biblical Book of 23, 41; guilt, Ego development and 27–8; history, personal and collective 29; "iconic constancy," myth as 23; *in illo tempore* ('in that time') 22, 23, 24; *imago Dei* 42; individuation 42–3; infancy, syntony between inner and outer worlds of 30; integration of the four modalities 38; Japan, separation of Ego from unconscious in 27; Jesus Christ 41–2; *kairòs, kronos* and 31; Kronos-Saturn 21; *Memories, Dreams, Reflections* (Jung, C.G.) 32, 37; *Midnight in Paris* (Woody Allen film) 33; modalities of temporality xiii; mother and infant, synchronistic match-ups between 31; mystical conjunction 37; myth as achronistic temporality 23; neuroscience, "episodic memory" and 25–6; New Testament 41–2; nostalgia, dyschronicity and 33; "original sin" 23; Platonic year 40–41; psychological temporality, achronicity and 21; "reality principle," Ego and 28–9; regression therapy, exploration of 36; religion, release from modalities of temporality and 42–3; retro-fantasizing *(zurückphantasieren)* 28; seasons, changing of 21; "semantic consciousness" 28; shame, achronicity and 25; shame, early and preverbal experience of 30–31; shame, humility and 38; shame, temporality and development of 35–6; shame and guilt, transformation of 36–7; shame and temporality, psychological connection between 19; shame-cultures, guilt and 28; shame in human experience 43; synchronicity 20, 22, 29–31, 32, 35, 37, 38; synchronicity, temporality and 22; temporality, levels of 40; temporality as chronicity 20–21; temporality systems, convergence of 35–6; time, concept of 19–20; time, human sense of 23–4; *Time, Rhythm and Repose* (Von Franz, M.-L.) 40; transcendent function, role of 37–43; transgenerational transmissions 37; transpersonal sources 38; trauma, transgenerational transmission of 36; trauma of being a Jew in Nazi Germany 36–7; unification, conjunction and 37; wartime experience of Jung, temporality and 32–3

theoretical physics, revolution in 2
Tilliach, P. 42
time: concept of 19–20; dual dimension of 17–18; evil and dimension of xiii; human sense of 23–4; notions of xi, 90; time reversal 6, 85

Time, Rhythm and Repose (Von Franz, M.-L.) 40
time dimensions, comparison between Panikkar and Jung on: bereavement, time and 17–18; causality and synchronicity, inextricably interwoven dimensions of 15; consciousness, fostering a symbolic attitude to 16; creativity, causality and 15–16; eternity 15; eternity, present as temporal dimension of 17; historical inertia, destiny and 16; human consciousness 15–16; intellect, discriminating faculty of 15; *kairòs* 15; *kairòs, kronos* and 17, 18; Oedipus, myth of 16–17; Psyche, subjective responsibility for destiny and 16; reality, discontinuous nature of 16; rhizome, life and 18; Self, Jungian sense of 15; "tempiternity" 15; time. dual dimension of 17–18
timelessness 1, 19, 21, 27, 40–41, 72, 92
Tiresias 17
tonality, levels of 91
transcendent function: Jung's notion of 74; role of 37–43
transformation 11, 61, 65, 66, 81, 82, 92–3; maturative transformation 83; transformative bonds 12; transformative effects 1
transgenerational transmissions 36, 37
transpersonal sources 38
trauma: of being Jewish in Nazi Germany 36–7; temporal

dimension of xiv–xv; transgenerational transmission of 36
Trevi, M. 82
Trevi, M. and Romano, A. 54
Turbulent Times, Creative Minds. (Neumann, E. and Jung. C.G.) 55

unconsciousness 71–2; root of all evil 58
understanding 86, 87, 90
unification, conjunction and 37
"The Experience of the Unitary Reality" (Neumann, E.) 6–7

Van Erkelens, H. 1, 9
Van Erkelens, H. and Wiegel, F.W. 6, 11
Vermeer, J. xii
Vienna, Captain in 66, 86, 87
Von Franz, M.-L. 1, 11, 12, 74; temporality, modalities of, problem of shame and 20, 21, 31, 40

wartime experience of Jung, temporality and 32–3
White, S.A. 83
white keys xi, 88–9; as words, black keys as meaning 6
wholeness 93
words 85, 86–7, 89, 90, 91, 92; but not meaning, school of understanding of 85; meaning and xvi, 6
World Council of Churches 63

Yahweh, myth of 61, 66, 67, 68–9
Yiassemides, A. 19, 22